Cicero. De Natura Deorum, Tr., With Notes
By H. Owgan

KELLY'S KEYS TO THE CLASSICS.

KELLY'S

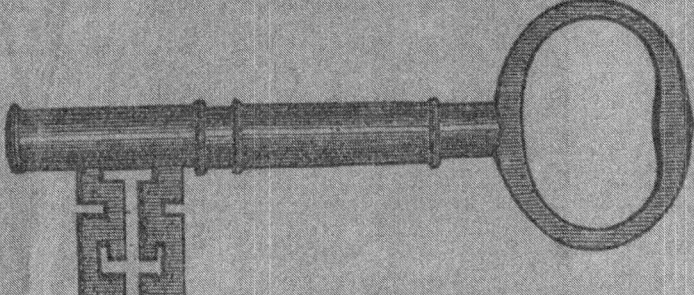

TO

CICERO'S
NATURE OF THE GODS.

Complete.

A LITERAL TRANSLATION

BY

HENRY OWGAN, L.L.D

Kelly's Keys to the ....s.

CORNEILLE'S Cinna. Lit. trans. by Roscoe Mongan, B.A.- 1 6
CORNEILLE'S Le Cid. Lit. trans. by Roscoe Mongan, B.A. 1 6
CORNEILLE'S Horace. Lit. trans. by Roscoe Mongan, B.A. 1 6
MOLIERE'S Le Malade Imaginaire. By R. Mongan, B.A. - 1 6
RACINE'S Athalie. Lit. trans. by Roscoe Mongan, B.A.   - 1 6
RACINE'S Esther. Literally translated by Rev. J. Rice   - 1 6

London: JAMES CORNISH AND SONS, 297, High Holborn, W.C.
and 37, Lord St., and 42, North John St., Liverpool.
C. COMBRIDGE, 18, Grafton St., Dublin.

Kelly's Keys to the Classics.

Literal English Translations of the Latin and Greek Classics.

For the use of Teachers and Students.

BOOK POST.—Any of these Keys will be sent by Post for Two Stamps extra. Orders by Post must be accompanied by Stamps or Post Office Order, and will receive immediate attention.

Specimen of Kelly's Keys to the Classics.

FROM CÆSAR'S GALLIC WAR. BY J. B. OWGAN.

"All Gaul is divided into three parts, of which the Belgæ inhabit one, the Aquitani another; those who in their own language are called Celtæ, in ours, Gauls, a third. All these differ among themselves in language, institutions, laws."

LATIN.

	s. d.
CÆSAR'S Gallic War (Books 1 to 4). Literally translated by J. B. Owgan	1 6
—— (Books 5, 6, 7). Literally translated by C. W. Bateman	1 6
—— (Complete). Lit. translated by Owgan and Bateman	2 6
CICERO On Old Age and Friendship. Translated by W. Lewers	1 0
—— Offices. Literally translated by Henry Owgan, LL.D.	2 0
—— In Verrem. Literally translated by R. Mongan, B.A.	1 6
—— Against Catiline. Literally translated by R. Mongan	1 6
—— Pro Milone. Literally translated by Roscoe Mongan, B.A.	1 6
—— Pro Lege Manilia. Literally translated by Roscoe Mongan, B.A.	1 0
—— Divinatio (against Quintus Cæcilius). Lit. translated by R. Mongan	1 6
—— Pro Murena. Literally translated by Roscoe Mongan, B.A.	1 6
—— Pro S. Roscio. Literally translated by T. J. Arnold	1 6
—— On the Nature of Gods. Literally translated by H. Owgan, LL.D.	
HORACE (Complete). By H. Owgan, LL.D. and R. Mongan	2 6
—— (Satires and Epistles). By Owgan and Mongan	1 6
—— (Odes, Epodes, and Carmen Seculare). By H. Owgan, LL.D.	1 6
LIVY (Books 1 to 3). Literally translated by Roscoe Mongan	2 6
—— (Books 4 and 5). Literally translated by Lewers and M'Devitt	2 6
—— (Book 21). (Book 22). Lit. trans. by T. J. Arnold ... each	1 6
—— (Book 23). (Book 24). Lit. trans. by Roscoe Mongan, B.A. ,,	1 6
OVID'S Fasti (Books 1 to 3). Literally translated by Roscoe Mongan	2 0
—— (Books 4, 5, 6). Literally translated by Roscoe Mongan, B.A.	2 0
—— (Complete). Literally translated by Roscoe Mongan, B.A.	3 6
—— Heroides (Ep. 1 to 12). Literally translated by Roscoe Mongan, B.A.	2 0
—— Metamorphoses (Books 1 to 3). Literally translated by R. Mongan	1 6
—— (Books 4 and 5). Literally translated by R. Mongan	1 6
—— Epistolæ ex Ponto (Books 1 and 2). Lit. translated by R. Mongan	1 6
—— (Books 3 and 4). Lit. translated by R. Mongan	1 6
—— Tristia (Book 1). Literally translated by R. Mongan, B.A.	
PLAUTUS Menæchmi. Literally translated by H. Owgan, LL.D.	1 6
—— Trinummus. Literally translated by H. Owgan, LL.D.	1 6
SALLUST'S Histories, Catiline and Jugurtha (Complete.) By H. Owgan	2 0
—— Catiline. Literally translated by H. Owgan, LL.D.	1 0
—— Jugurtha. Literally translated by H. Owgan, LL.D.	1 6
TACITUS' Annals (Books 1 to 6). By R. Mongan, B.A.	2 6
—— Germany and Agricola. By H. Owgan, LL.D.	1 6
—— NCE'S Adelphi. Literally translated by Roscoe Mongan, B.A.	1 6
—— Self Tormentor. Literally translated by Roscoe Mongan, B.A.	1 6
—— Phormio. Literally translated by Roscoe Mongan, B.A.	1 6

KELLY'S KEYS TO THE CLASSICS.
LITERAL ENGLISH TRANSLATIONS OF THE LATIN AND GREEK CLASSICS.

GREEK.

	s.	d.
ÆSCHINES against Ctesiphon, and Demosthenes on the Crown. Literally translated by Roscoe Mongan, B.A.	2	0
ÆSCHYLUS' Prometheus Vinctus. Lit. trans. by R. Mongan	1	0
ÆSCHYLUS' The Seven against Thebes. Lit. trans. by R. Mongan	1	0
DEMOSTHENES' Phillipics. Lit. trans. by H. Owgan	1	0
DEMOSTHENES' Olynthiacs. Lit. trans. by H. Owgan	1	0
DEMOSTHENES on the Crown, and Æschines. By R. Mongan	2	0
EURIPIDES' Medea. Literally translated by R. Mongan, B.A.	1	0
EURIPIDES' Hecuba. Literally translated by R. Mongan, B.A.	1	0
EURIPIDES' Phœnissæ. Lit. trans. by R. Mongan, B.A.	1	0
EURIPIDES' Alcestis. Lit. trans. by Roscoe Mongan, B.A.	1	0
EURIPIDES' Ion. Lit. trans. by Roscoe Mongan, B.A.	1	6
EURIPIDES' Iphigenia in Aulis. Lit. trans. by T. J. Arnold	1	6
EURIPIDES. The Troades. Lit. translated by T. J. Arnold	1	6
HOMER'S Iliad (Books 1 to 8). Lit. trans. by C. W. Bateman	2	0
HOMER'S Iliad (Books 1 to 4). Trans. by C. W. Bateman	1	6
HOMER'S Iliad (Books 5 to 8). By C.W. Bateman	1	6
HOMER'S Iliad (Books 9 to 12). Lit. trans. by R. Mongan	1	6
HOMER'S Iliad (Books 13 to 16). Lit. trans. by R. Mongan	1	6
HOMER'S Iliad (Books 17 to 20). Lit. trans. by R. Mongan	1	6
HOMER'S Iliad (Books 21 to 24). Lit. trans. by R. Mongan	1	6
HOMER'S Odyssey (Books 1 to 6). Lit. trans. by R. Mongan	2	0
HOMER'S Odyssey (Books 7 to 12). Lit. trans. by R. Mongan	2	0
HOMER'S Odyssey (Books 13 to 18). Lit. trans. by R. Mongan	2	0
HOMER'S Odyssey (Books 19 to 24). Lit. trans. by R. Mongan	2	0
ISOCRATES' Panegyric. Lit. trans. by Rev. J. Rice	2	0
PLATO. The Apology of Socrates and Crito, with the Phædo. Literally translated by J. Eccleston, B.A.	2	0
SOPHOCLES' Œdipus Tyrannus. Lit. trans. by R. Mongan	1	0
SOPHOCLES' Antigone. Lit. trans. by Roscoe Mongan, B.A.	1	0
SOPHOCLES' Ajax. Lit. trans. by Roscoe Mongan, B.A.	1	0
SOPHOCLES' Philoctetes. Literally translated by R. Mongan	1	0
XENOPHON'S Anabasis (Books 1 to 3). By T. J. Arnold	1	6
XENOPHON'S Anabasis (Books 4 and 5). By T. J. Arnold	1	6
XENOPHON'S Anabasis (Books 6 and 7). By T. J. Arnold	1	6
XENOPHON'S Anabasis (Complete). Lit. trans. by T. J. Arnold	3	6
XENOPHON'S Hellenics (Books 1 to 3). Literally translated	2	0
XENOPHON'S Cyropædia (Books 1, 2, 3). By R. Mongan	2	0
XENOPHON'S Cyropædia (Books 4, 5, 6). Literally translated	2	0
XENOPHON'S Cyropædia (Books 7 and 8). Literally translated	2	0
XENOPHON'S Agesilaus. Lit. trans. by R. Mongan, B.A.	2	0

Kelly's Keys to the French Classics.

	s.	d.
CORNEILLE'S Cinna. Lit. trans. by Roscoe Mongan, B.A.	1	6
CORNEILLE'S Le Cid. Lit. trans. by Roscoe Mongan, B.A.	1	6
CORNEILLE'S Horace. Lit. trans. by Roscoe Mongan, B.A.	1	6
MOLIERE'S Le Malade Imaginaire. By R. Mongan, B.A.	1	6
RACINE'S Athalie. Lit. trans. by Roscoe Mongan, B.A.	1	6
RACINE'S Esther. Literally translated by Rev. J. Rice	1	6

London: JAMES CORNISH AND SONS, 297, High Holborn, W.C.
and 37, Lord St., and 42, North John St., Liverpool.
C. COMBRIDGE, 18, Grafton St., Dublin.

KELLY'S KEYS TO THE CLASSICS.

LITERAL ENGLISH TRANSLATIONS OF THE LATIN AND GREEK CLASSICS.

BOOK POST.—Any of these Keys will be sent by Post for Two Stamps extra. Orders by Post must be accompanied by Stamps or Post Office Order, and will receive immediate attention.

LATIN.

	s.	d.
CÆSAR'S Gallic War (Books 1 to 4). By J. B. Owgan, B.A.	1	6
CÆSAR'S Gallic War (Books 5, 6, 7). By C. W. Bateman	1	6
CÆSAR'S Gallic War (Complete). By Owgan and Bateman	2	6
CICERO'S Cato Major and Lælius. On Old Age and Friendship	1	0
CICERO'S Offices. By Henry Owgan, LL.D.	2	0
CICERO In Verrem. Actio Prima. Lit. trans. by R. Mongan.	1	6
CICERO (against Catiline). Lit. trans. by R. Mongan	1	6
CICERO Pro Milone. Literally translated by R. Mongan, B.A.	1	6
CICERO Pro Lege Manilia. Lit. trans. by Roscoe Mongan, B.A.	1	0
CICERO'S Divinatio (against Quintus Cæcilius). By R. Mongan	1	6
CICERO Pro S. Roscio. Literally translated by T. J. Arnold	1	6
CICERO Pro Murena. Lit. trans. by Roscoe Mongan, B.A.	1	6
CICERO On the Nature of the Gods (Complete). Literally translated by H. Owgan, LL.D.	3	6
HORACE (Complete). By H. Owgan, LL.D., and R. Mongan	2	6
HORACE (Satires and Epistles). By Owgan and Mongan	1	6
HORACE (Odes, Epodes, and Carmen Seculare). By Owgan	1	6
JUVENAL'S Satires. Lit. trans. by R. Mongan, B.A. *(In the Press)*		
LIVY (Books 1 to 3). Lit. trans. by Roscoe Mongan	2	6
LIVY (Books 4 and 5). Lit. trans. by Lewers and M'Devitt	2	6
LIVY (Book 21). Literally translated by T. J. Arnold	1	6
LIVY (Book 22). Literally translated by T. J. Arnold	1	6
LIVY (Book 23). Literally translated by Roscoe Mongan, B.A.	1	6
LIVY (Book 24). Literally translated by Roscoe Mongan, B.A.	1	6
OVID'S Fasti (Books 1 to 3). Lit. trans. by Roscoe Mongan	2	0
OVID'S Fasti (Books 4, 5 and 6). Lit. trans. by R. Mongan	2	0
OVID'S Fasti (Complete). Lit. trans. by R. Mongan	3	6
OVID'S Heroides (Ep. 1 to 13). Lit. trans. by R. Mongan, B.A.	2	0
OVID'S Epistolæ ex Ponto (Books 1 and 2). By R. Mongan	1	6
OVID'S Epistolæ ex Ponto (Books 3 and 4). By R. Mongan	1	6
OVID'S Metamorphoses (Books 1 to 3). Lit. trans. by R. Mongan	1	6
OVID'S Metamorphoses (Bks. 4 and 5). Lit. trans. by R. Mongan	1	6
PLAUTUS' Menæchmi. Lit. trans. by H. Owgan, LL.D	1	6
PLAUTUS' Trinummus. Lit. trans. by H. Owgan, LL.D.	1	6
SALLUST'S Catiline. Lit. trans. by H. Owgan, LL.D.	1	0
SALLUST'S Jugurtha. Lit. trans. by H. Owgan, LL.D.	1	6
SALLUST'S Histories, Catiline and Jugurtha. By H. Owgan	2	0
TACITUS' Annals (Books 1 to 6). By R. Mongan, B.A.	2	6
TACITUS' Germany and Agricola. By H. Owgan, LL.D.	1	6
TERENCE'S Andria. Lit. trans. by R. Mongan, B.A.	1	6
TERENCE'S Adelphi. Lit. trans. by Roscoe Mongan, B.A.	1	6
TERENCE'S Heautontimorumenos (The Self-Tormentor) ditto	1	6
TERENCE'S Hecyra. Lit. trans. by R. Mongan, B.A. *(In the Press)*		
VIRGIL'S Bucolics and Georgics. Lit. trans. by R. Mongan, B.A.	1	6
VIRGIL'S Æneid (Books 1 to 6). Lit. trans. by H. Owgan, LL.D.	1	6
VIRGIL'S Æneid (Books 7 to 12). Lit. trans. by R. Mongan, B.A.	1	6
VIRGIL'S Whole Works. Lit. trans. by Owgan and Mongan	2	6
VIRGIL'S Æneid (Book 1). Completely parsed, giving the meaning, derivation, person, number, case, gender, mood, voice, etc., of every word	1	6

KELLY'S KEYS TO THE CLASSICS.

CICERO DE NATURA DEORUM.

(CICERO ON THE NATURE OF THE GODS.)

COMPLETE.

Literally Translated.

WITH NOTES ON THE LOGIC, ASTRONOMY, ETC.

BY

H. OWGAN, LL.D.

FORMERLY UNIVERSITY SCHOLAR, AND SENIOR MODERATOR IN CLASSICS, T.C.D.

LONDON:
JAMES CORNISH & SONS, 297, HIGH HOLBORN.
LIVERPOOL: 37, LORD STREET, AND 42, NORTH JOHN STREET.
DUBLIN: C. COMBRIDGE, 18, GRAFTON STREET.

CICERO: DE NATURA DEORUM.

BOOK I.

1. WHILE many subjects in philosophy are far from being as yet sufficiently explained, Brutus, the inquiry respecting the nature of Gods, especially, is, as you well know, extremely difficult and obscure, as it is, at the same time, most fascinating for metaphysical study, and indispensable to the repression of superstition. Of this the views of the most learned men are so various and conflicting that it ought to be a convincing proof that the cause, that is, the first principle of philosophy, is want of knowledge; and that the Academics have prudently withheld their consent from uncertainties. For, what can be more disreputable than impulsiveness, or what so impulsive and unsuited to the seriousness and consistency of a philosopher, as either to entertain false opinions, or without hesitation to uphold what is not sufficiently investigated and ascertained? as for instance, in this inquiry, the great majority have said that there are Gods, which is most probable, and the belief to which we are all led by intuition for our guide: Pythagoras says that he has his doubts; and Diagoras of Melos and Theodorus of Cyrene were of opinion that they have no existence. Those, however, who have affirmed the existence of Gods are so various and contradictory, that it would be tiresome to enumerate their opinions; because, respecting the forms of Gods and their localities and habitations and modes of life, many statements are made, and these are subjects of the widest differences among philosophers; but the question which most of all involves the subject and the argument—whether they do nothing, design nothing, are exempt from all concern and government

of the universe, or, on the other hand, all things have been originally made and arranged and are governed and kept in motion by them to all eternity—is the most important controversy; and unless it is decided, people must inevitably be under the strongest delusion, and live in ignorance of the most important facts.

2. For there are and have been philosophers who believed that the Gods take no interest in human affairs : and if their theory is true, what devotion, what holiness, what religion can there be ? For all these attributes are to be, in their genuine essence, assigned to the power of the Gods, only on condition that they are recognised by them, and that something is done for mankind by immortal Gods. But, if the Gods have neither the power nor the will to help us, and take no interest whatever in us, nor notice how we are, and there is nothing that can be imparted by them to human life, what reason is there why we should address any worship, honours, or prayers to immortal Gods ? But, in an imaginary and illusive form, devotion, like other virtues, can have no place; and with this, holiness and religion must, of necessity, disappear; and on the removal of these, derangement of life and much irregularity ensue— and I am not sure that, on the extinction of devotion to the Gods, truth, also, and human fellowship, and especially that most excellent virtue, justice, will not be abolished. There are, however, other philosophers, and these great and distinguished, who believe that the whole universe is administered and governed by the intellect and reason of the Gods; and not that only, but that human life is the object of their wisdom and providence; for they suppose that the crops and other products of the earth—and the weather—and succession of seasons and varieties of climate, by which all that the earth produces comes to reproductive maturity, are the gifts of the immortal Gods to mankind; and enumerate many instances which shall be mentioned in these pages, and are of such a sort that the immortal Gods would almost seem to have been actually formed for the benefit of men. In reply to these Carneades adduces so many arguments, that he instigates all who are not apathetic to a desire of examining the truth : for there is no subject on which not only the ignorant, but scholars, so obstinately differ. And as all these opinions are so various and irreconcilable, it is possible, on the one hand, that none of them

may be true, but on the other, impossible that more than one can be so.

3. In this argument, however, we can at the same time conciliate friendly disputants and refute jealous antagonists; so that the latter may regret their censure and the former find pleasure in having improved their knowledge—for friendly advisers should be instructed and hostile assailants kept at a distance. I find, however, that much has resulted from those many essays which we have published within a short time, and various discussions by some who wonder whence this recent industry in writing has come to us; and others anxious to know what certainty we have attained on the several subjects. I have observed, also, that to many persons it seems strange that the philosophy which blots out the light, and casts a sort of darkness over everything, should have, more than any other, recommended itself to us; and that the patronage of a doctrine forsaken and long since abandoned should be unexpectedly adopted by us. We have however, neither suddenly begun to cultivate philosophy nor from our earliest years devoted a merely ordinary share of time and trouble to that study; and when we seemed to be least, were in reality most philosophic, as the speeches prove, full of the maxims of philosophers, and our intimacy with the most accomplished men, for which our house has been always distinguished, and those masters, Diodotus, Philo, Antiochus and Poseidonius, by whom we have been taught; and if all the lessons of philosophy are applied in practice, we believe that in political and personal transactions we have performed what reason and learning required.

4. If, however, anyone wishes to know what motive urged us at so late a time to commit all this to writing, there is nothing that we can so easily explain. When, for instance, we were weary of idleness, and the condition of the Republic was such, that it was inevitable that it should be governed by the wisdom and diligence of a single ruler, it occurred to me that, principally in the interest of the Republic, philosophy should be made plain to the men of our time, believing it a matter of much importance to the honour and glory of the State, that subjects so serious and celebrated should be embodied in Latin writings also: and I am so much the less dissatisfied with my intention, as I can easily perceive how many I have encouraged to the pursuit, not only of learning, but even of writing; because many men instructed in Greek

learning were unable to impart what they had learned to their countrymen, because they doubted that what they had heard from Greeks could be expressed in Latin—and in that particular we seem to have advanced so far that we are not surpassed by Greeks, even in the resources of language; mental suffering, also, produced by great and oppressive injustice of fortune, has urged me to resort to this course; though, if I could find any more effectual relief, I would not have addressed myself especially to this; and even from this I could derive no greater enjoyment than by devoting myself not only to the study of books, but to the exposition of philosophy in general —all its branches, in fact, and all its elements, are most easily known when the questions are fully stated in writing—because there is a wonderful succession and connection of subjects, so that they seem all joined in successive order, and fitted and bound up together.

5. Those who inquire what our own opinion is on every subject, exhibit more curiosity than is necessary; because it is not authority that is to be regarded in discussion, so much as the weight of argument. And still further, as a general rule, the authority of those who profess to teach, is a hindrance to those who want to learn; for they cease to apply their own judgment, and accept as a certainty whatever they see decided by the man whom they follow. Nor, indeed, do I generally approve of what we are told of the Pythagoreans; for they say that, when they were asked, respecting what they asserted in controversy, why it was so, they usually replied, 'He said so himself.' Himself was, of course, Pythagoras. Such was the influence of a prejudged opinion, that authority without argument was supreme. To those, however, who wonder that we have adopted this doctrine in particular, a sufficient answer seems to be given in these four academic treatises. Nor is it the advocacy of forsaken and exploded subjects that we have taken up; because, with the death of men, opinions do not also die; but they sometimes feel the want of the light of authority, as, for instance, this philosophic system of arguing against everything and deciding nothing definitely, originating with Socrates, continued by Arcesilas and established by Carneades, has flourished down to our time; though I understand that, even in Greece, it is at present almost deserted. And this I believe to have resulted not from any fault of the Academy, but of human stupidity; for if it is difficult to understand

individual doctrines, how much more to understand all ? And yet, this is what they must do whose intention is to speak for and against all philosophers, for the discovery of truth. Of this so important and difficult a performance I do not profess to have attained the power, but maintain that I have sought it. Nor, at the same time, is it possible that those who cultivate this system of philosophy have nothing to follow. This subject has been, once for all, more carefully discussed in another place; but as some men are slow to learn and stupid, they seem to need frequent reminding. For we are not men who think nothing true, but who assert that in every truth there is some alloy of error with so close a resemblance, that there is no visible mark for decision and acquiescence. And herefrom arises this fact, that there are many probabilities that, although not ascertained, still have a certain aspect of such distinction and clearness that the life of a wise man should be governed by them.

6. Now, in order to free myself from all misunderstanding, I will state fairly the views of philosophers respecting the nature of Gods. And, under this head, it seems necessary to summon together all who may determine which of them is true. Then, and then only, will the Academy seem to me impertinent, if either all are unanimous, or some one shall be found who has discovered what is the truth; so that I may exclaim, quoting from the Synephebi, 'I call, I demand, I beg, pray, invoke and beseech the honour of Gods, fellow-citizens and all young men;' not in a trifling case, as that man complains that 'capital crimes are committed in the State—a courtesan refuses to take money from a loving friend;' but that they may come forward, ascertain and take notice what should be thought of religion, devotion, holiness, ritual, honour, oaths; of temples, shrines, periodical sacrifices, and even of the auguries over which we ourselves hold office. For all these are to be included in this inquiry respecting immortal Gods. Such variety of doctrine among most learned men, on a most important subject, will, of course, suggest further doubts even to those who believe that they hold any truth whatever. This I have observed on many other occasions; but most of all when a careful, sincere and elaborate discussion respecting immortal Gods took place at the house of my friend, C. Cotta. For when, during the Latin holidays, I visited him at his own request and invitation, I found him sitting in his study arguing

with C. Velleius, the senator, to whom, at that time, the Epicureans assigned the first place among the men of our day. Q. Lucilius Balbus was there also, who was so far advanced in Stoic doctrine that he was compared to the most eminent Greeks in that particular. Then said Cotta, as soon as he saw me, 'You come just in time. I am holding a discussion with Velleius on an interesting question, in which, considering your tastes, it will not be out of your way to take part.'.

7. 'It seems to me, too,' I said, 'that I have come in time, for you three here assembled are the champions of three doctrines. If M. Piso was here, no chair would be empty for any philosophy; that is, of those in repute.' Then said Cotta: 'If the treatise of our friend Antiochus, recently sent by him to Balbus, tells the truth, there is no occasion to regret the absence of your friend Piso—because the Stoics and Peripatetics seem to agree in substance with Antiochus, though differing in form: and I should like to know, Balbus, what you think of that essay.' 'I?' said he; 'I am surprised that Antiochus, so very sharp a man, did not perceive that there is a very wide difference between the Stoics, who distinguished honour from expediency, not merely in name, but in its nature generally, and the Peripatetics, who so far identify honour and expediency, that they differ only in extent and, so to speak, in degree, and not in kind—for this is not a small verbal, but an important practical distinction. But of this hereafter. Now, to our present business, if you please.' 'I think so,' said Cotta; 'but, in order that our friend, who has just joined us'—looking at me—'may be made aware of our subject: we were talking of the nature of Gods; and, as the question seemed to me, as usual, extremely obscure, I was inquiring of Velleius respecting the opinion of Epicurus. For this reason, Velleius, if not too tiresome, repeat what you have been saying.' 'I will repeat it, certainly, though he comes to help not me but you, for both of you'—he added, with a smile—'have learned from Philo to know nothing.' Then said I: 'What we have learned is for Cotta to say, but I object to your assuming that I came to help him; but merely as a hearer, and an impartial one, with freedom of judgment, and tied down by no association of such a sort that, whether I will or not, I must support a certain doctrine.'

8. Then said Velleius, with the perfect confidence usually

displayed by men of that sect generally, and dreading nothing so much as the appearance of having a doubt on any subject, as if he had just come down from the council of the Gods and the interstellar spaces of Epicurus: 'Hear, not of empty and imaginary doctrines, not of a mechanic and architect of the universe, the God of Plato's Timæus, nor of a fortune-telling crone, the Pronœa of the Stoics, which we may call in Latin Providence; nor, in fact, of the world itself, endowed with senses and intellect, a circular, fiery revolving God—all monsters and miracles of philosophers who do not reason, but dream. With what mental vision could your master, Plato, have seen the great laboratory of such a work? What were the building, the implements, the scaffold, the engines, and the workmen of so great a task? How could air, fire, water, and earth listen to and obey the will of the architect? Whence came those five *elements*, of which others are formed, conveniently taking their places for the production of intellect and the formation of senses? It would be tedious to mention all, for they look as if they were desired rather than discovered. But this is the great absurdity, that he who represents the world as being not only produced, but almost manufactured, says also that it will be eternal. Can you believe that he has had the smallest taste, as they say, of physiology —that is, the science of nature—who supposes that anything originated can be eternal? What combination, for instance, is inseparable, or, what is there that has a beginning and no end? But if that Pronœa of yours exists, Lucilius, I want, as I said just now, the agents, the engines, the whole plan and arrangement of the entire work; but if it is any other power, why did it make a world perishable, not, as Plato's God, eternal?

9. 'From both of you I wish to know why the architects of the world suddenly came forward, after having slept through countless ages; because the ages must have been, though the world was not. I am now speaking not of the ages which consist of a number of days and nights and annual revolutions—for I admit that these could not be reckoned without the revolutions of the globe—but there was an eternity of limitless duration which no calculation of time could measure. What that was in duration cannot be conceived, as it cannot be imagined that there ever was a time when time had no existence. During all that immeasurable time then, I ask you, Balbus, why your Pronœa was idle?

Was it the trouble that it was avoiding? But that cannot affect a God; nor was there any, since all the elements—air, fire, earth and sea—were obedient to the Deity. And what reason was there why a God should desire to embellish the world with a zodiac of luminous bodies, as if he were an ædile? If it was in order to have a better dwelling for himself, he must, of course, during all preceding time, have lived in darkness, as if in a dungeon. Are we to suppose that thenceforth he was gratified by the variety with which we see sky and earth embellished? What enjoyment could that be to a God? If it could, he could not have done so long without it. Were all these arrangements made, as you generally assert, by the Deity for the sake of men? Of philosophers? Then so great a structure was made in the interest of a few. Of the ignorant? But, in the first place, there was no motive to bestow favours on the unworthy; secondly, what did he gain? Since all the ignorant are unquestionably most miserable—for what can we call more miserable than ignorance? Still further is the fact that there is so much suffering in life, that philosophers mitigate it by compensating enjoyments, while the ignorant can neither avoid it in the future nor endure it in the present.

10. 'Those, again, who have affirmed that the world itself has life and intelligence, have never known what shape an intelligent mind could assume; but of this I will speak presently. I will just now only wonder at the stupidity of those men who suppose that a being, at the same time immortal and happy, can be round; because Plato says that no figure can surpass that in beauty. But to me that of a cylinder, or a cube, or a cone, or a pyramid, seems more beautiful. But, what sort of life is assigned to that circular God? Apparently a revolution of such speed that nothing like it can be even imagined; and in that I cannot see where a permanently uniform intellect and a happy life can find a place; and why should not that which would be irksome in our life, if exhibited in the smallest degree, be regarded as an inconvenience to a God also? The earth, for instance, being a portion of the world, is part, also, of the Deity; and yet we see most extensive regions of the earth uninhabitable and uncultivated, because some of them are burnt up by the proximity of the sun, and some are frozen by snow and frost from the long distance of the sun; and, if the world is God, as these are portions of the world, the limbs of the God must be

described as partly scorching and partly freezing. Such is your theory, Lucilius; but for the nature of the others I will go back to the earliest of our predecessors. Thales of Miletus, for instance, who was the first to investigate this subject, said that water was the beginning of everything, and the Deity the intellect that formed all things of water. If God can exist without sensation and intellect, and if intellect can exist by itself independently of matter, why has he combined water with intellect?

The theory of Anaximander, on the other hand, is that Gods can be born, beginning and ceasing to exist at long intervals, and that there are countless worlds. But how can we imagine a God otherwise than immortal? Still later, Anaximenes decided that the air is God: that it has a beginning and is boundless and infinite, and in perpetual motion; as if the shapeless air could be a God, especially when a God should have not only some form, but one of perfect beauty, or as if liability to death were not a condition of everything that has a beginning.

11. 'After him, Anaxagoras, who received his doctrine from Anaximenes, was the first who determined that the plan and method of the universe was drawn out and completed by the power and wisdom of an infinite intellect. But in this theory he did not see that motion, continuous and combined with sensation, cannot exist in the Infinite—or any sensation whatever to the impact of which Nature itself would not be sensitive; and further, if he meant that intellect to be some sort of animal, there must be something intrinsic from which it would take a name. But what can be more intrinsic than intellect? It must, then, be clothed in an external body. But, as this is not his opinion, an immaterial and uniform intellect, having nothing attached to it through which it could be sensitive, seems to defy the perceptive power of our understanding. Alcmæon of Crotona, on the other hand, who attributed a divine essence to the sun and moon and other sidereal bodies, and even to mind, did not perceive that he was attributing immortality to mortal things. For Pythagoras, who taught that there is diffused through all nature, coming and going, a mind, from which our minds emanate, did not perceive that by division into human minds the Deity would be dismembered and torn asunder; and, as our minds are unhappy—which is the condition of most of us—that a portion of the Deity must be unhappy, which is im-

possible. Why, again, should the human mind be ignorant of anything, if it were God; and, further, how could that God, if it were nothing but mind, be either diffused through, or inherent in the world? Then Xenophanes, whose theory was that, with the addition of intellect, everything besides that was infinite was God, is open to the same objection as the others on the question of intellect; and still more on the subject of infinity, in which nothing sentient can be coexistent. For Parmenides, in fact, constructs an imaginary something like a diadem—which he calls *Stephané*—enclosing in a fiery ring a globe of light encircling the sky, and this he calls God, in whom no one can detect divine form or perception; and many other deformities of the same kind, inasmuch as he attributes to God desire, and other such emotions, which are effaced by sickness or sleep, or forgetfulness, or time; and the same doctrine respecting the stars, which may be omitted in his case, as it has been refuted in our review of another.

12. 'Empedocles, also, while guilty of many other errors, fails most discreditably in his estimate of the Gods; for he maintains that the four elements, of which he believes that all things consist, are divine; though it is evident that they can be produced and destroyed, and are totally destitute of perception. Nor, in fact, does Protagoras, who professes to know nothing certain about Gods—whether they exist or not, or what they are like—seem to conjecture anything of their nature. Well, then? Does not Democritus, who sometimes includes in the number of Gods prototypes and their periodic movements; sometimes that creative power which gives off and sends out those prototypes; and, again, our own knowledge and understanding, labour under the greatest mistakes? And when, at the same time, he utterly denies that anything can be eternal, because nothing remains unchanged, does he not so far annihilate the Deity as to leave no conception of him remaining?

Well? As to the air, which Diogenes of Apollonia employs as a God—what perception or divine form can that have? Now, the inconsistency of Plato it would be tedious to discuss, because in the Timæus he denies that the father of this universe can be indicated by name; while in his treatise on *Laws*, he is of opinion that the personality of the Deity should not be the subject of any inquiry whatever. But, as to his idea of a God without a material body—what the

Greeks call *asomaton*—what that means it is impossible to understand, because it must of course be destitute of sensation; it must be also incapable of thought and of enjoyment; and we include all these in our conception of a God. He says, also, in the Timæus and in the *Laws*, that the world is God, and the sky and stars, and the earth, and our souls, and those, also, whom we have received in the religion of our ancestors, which are all, in themselves, manifestly false, and totally inconsistent with each other. And Xenophanes also, though in fewer words, makes nearly the same mistakes: for he represents Socrates, in his reported discourses, as arguing that the form of the Deity should not be a subject of inquiry, and at the same time speaking of the sun, and of mind, as God, and sometimes of one, and then of several Gods—which are among the same mistakes, very nearly, that we have found in Plato.

13. 'Antisthenes, too, in that treatise called *Physicus*, by saying that the Gods of the people are many, and the God of Nature one—destroys the power and character of Gods. Very nearly to the same extent, Speusippus, following his uncle Plato, and speaking of a force, and that a living force, by which the universe is governed, endeavours to eradicate from the mind all idea of Gods. Aristotle, in the third book of his philosophy, exhibits much inconsistency, though not differing from his teacher Plato; for sometimes he attributes all divinity to intellect; sometimes asserts that the world itself is God; sometimes sets up another ruler of the world, and assigns to him the duty of controlling and maintaining the motion of the world by a sort of revolution; and then speaks of the heat of the atmosphere as a God, not perceiving that the atmosphere is a portion of the world which he has elsewhere described as God. But how could that divine perception of the sphere be maintained under so rapid a revolution? And secondly, what becomes of all those Deities, if we include the atmosphere also as a God? When he implies, also, that God is incorporeal, he deprives him of all sensation and intelligence. And, still further, how could he, without a body, move the world? or how, if himself in perpetual motion, could he enjoy repose and happiness? Nor, indeed, is his fellow-student, Xenocrates, wiser in this particular, in whose works, treating of the nature of Gods, no likeness of a God is outlined. He says, for instance, that there are eight Gods; five who are classed as planets; one consisting of all

the fixed stars, as if one God could be supposed to be made up of scattered limbs; the sun he includes as the seventh, and the moon as the eighth; but through what perception these can be happy, it is impossible to conceive. Heraclides of Pontus, also of the school of Plato, has filled his works with childish legends, and supposes that the world and intellect, alternately, are divine. To the planets he attributes a divine nature, and depriving the Deity of sensation, decides that his form is changeable, and again, in the same treatise, classes the earth and sky among the Gods. But the inconsistency of Theophrastus is intolerable, for he attributes a divine supremacy sometimes to intellect, sometimes to the sky, and, again, to the stars of the Zodiac. Nor can one listen to his pupil Strato—who is called *Physicus*—who believes that all divine power dwells in phænomena of nature which includes the causes of production, growth and decay, but is destitute of all perception and form.

14. 'Zeno, on the other hand—that I may now come to your friends, Balbus—believes that the natural law is divine, and maintains its power by commanding what is right, and forbidding the opposite. But how he invests this law with life we cannot understand, for we certainly expect a God to be living. And yet, in another place, he alludes to the æther as a God—if one can imagine a God who perceives nothing and is never present with us, in our prayers and wishes and vows. In his other works, however, he signifies his opinion that a sort of intelligence, diffused through all physical creation, is gifted with divine power. He also assigns the same attribute to the stars, to the years, and the months and annual revolutions. But, in his explanation of Hesiod's *Theogonia* — that is, "the Birth of Gods" — he abolishes altogether the conventional and accepted ideas respecting them. For, he does not reckon among the Gods Jupiter, or Juno, or Vesta, or any other so called, but teaches us that these names are, in a certain sense, applied to lifeless and voiceless objects. Of his pupil Ariston, the theory is not less erroneous; for he does not believe either that the form of the Deity can be imagined, or that Gods have any sensation, and doubts whether or not the Deity has any life at all. Cleanthes, however, who was a hearer of Zeno's, together with the last named, says sometimes that the world itself is God; sometimes he gives that title to the intellect and soul of the entire creation; and then decides most con-

fidently that the most distant and vertical fire, surrounding externally, enclosing and encircling the whole universe, is God; and at the same time—as if raving—in the book which he wrote against pleasure, imagines, in one place, some sort of shape and visible aspect of Gods, elsewhere attributing all godhead to the stars; and again, decides that the God, whom our reason recognises, and of whom we desire to have an impression—so to speak—upon our consciousness, is never anywhere visible.

15. 'Persæus, also a pupil of Zeno, says that those persons by whom any facility for the improvement of society had been invented, have been regarded as Gods, and that the objects, which were useful and beneficial, were themselves indicated by the names of Gods; so that he says not merely that the inventions are due to Gods, but that they are themselves deified. And what can be more absurd than this elevation to divine honours of mean and unsightly things; or the deification of men long dead, all whose worship must consist in mourning? But Chrysippus, especially, who is considered the most ingenious interpreter of the dreams of the Stoics, collects a vast multitude of unknown Gods—so unknown, in fact, that we cannot, even by guessing, draw a rough sketch of them; though the human intellect is supposed to be able to imagine the form of anything. He says, for instance, that a divine essence belongs to reason and the mind and intellect of nature in general; that the world itself is God, and the all-pervading emanation of its mind; then, its own supremacy, which asserts itself in intellect and reason; and the general productive agency of creation, ubiquitous and comprising all things; then, the actual predestination and inevitable laws of future events, in addition to fire, and the æther which I have already mentioned; next, all things by nature fluid and spreading, such as water and earth and air, sun, moon, stars, the universe in which all things are contained, and even those men who have attained immortality. He argues, also, that the æther is what men call Jupiter; that the air diffused through the sea is Neptune; and the earth what is called Ceres; and on the same principle he disposes of the names of the rest of the Gods. He also asserts that a force of continuous and eternal law, which should be a sort of guide and teacher of life in moral obligations, is Jupiter, and speaks of the same as inevitable destiny, the eternal truth of the future; though of all these there is

not one so constituted, that a divine essence could be supposed to exist in it. All this is the subject of the first book on the nature of Gods : in the second, he proposes to reconcile the legends of Orpheus, Musæus, Hesiod, and Homer, to his own account of the immortal Gods in the first book ; so that even the most ancient poets, who never suspected any such doctrines, may appear to be Stoics. Following his example, Diogenes Babylonius, in the work entitled *Minerva*, transfers the birth of the Virgin and the maternity of Jupiter to physiology, and withdraws it altogether from mythology.

16. ' I have been illustrating not so much the theories of philosophers in general, as the dreams of lunatics : for, not much more irrational are those fables, which have been disseminated in the language of poets, and done mischief by their mere fascination ; where they have represented Gods fired with anger and maddened by lust, and have given us a view of their wars, battles, combats and wounds ; in addition to their hatreds, aversions, dissensions, births, deaths, complaints, lamentations, sensuality let loose in all excesses, adulteries, imprisonments, intrigues with human beings, and mortals begotten of immortals. With the fancies of the poets we may classify the wonders of magicians, and the follies of the Ægyptians in the same category ; and even the superstitions of the multitude, which are involved in the most obvious inconsistency and rejection of truth. Whoever reflects upon the folly and recklessness of these statements, must respect Epicurus, and include him in the number of those very beings who are the subject of the present inquiry : for it was he alone who perceived that originally Gods must exist, because instinct has itself stamped the recognition of them upon the minds of all men. For, what nation or race of men is there that has not, untaught, a presentiment of the existence of Gods ? This is what Epicurus calls *prolepsis* —that is, an intuition previously conceived by the mind, without which nothing can be understood, or investigated, or discussed. Of this principle we learn the power and utility from that divine work of Epicurus on the logic of inference.

17. ' You see, therefore, that the foundation of this inquiry is successfully laid ; for when a belief is established independently of ordinance or custom or law of any kind, and keeps its place as the firm and universal conviction of all men, it must be understood that Gods do exist, since we

have an implanted, or rather an inborn, perception of them. A fact, of which the intuitive belief of all men is identical, must be true. It must be admitted, then, that there are Gods. And, as this belief is generally uniform among all, not philosophers only, but even the unlearned, we must confess that this also is universally certain, that we have this intuition or transcendental perception of Gods—because new names must be found for new facts, as Epicurus gave the name of *prolepsis* to that which no one had previously so called.—We have, then, this perception, so that we believe the Gods to be happy and immortal. For the same intuition that has given us a primary perception of the existence of Gods, has also engraved upon our minds the belief of their immortality and happiness: and if this is so, that doctrine has been truly stated by Epicurus :—Whatever is happy and immortal, can neither have any trouble itself, nor inflict it upon another, and is, therefore, influenced neither by anger nor partiality: because everything so influenced is weak. If we desired nothing more than to worship the Gods devotedly, and to set ourselves free from superstition, enough would have been said; for the exalted nature of the Gods would be worshipped by man's devotion, in right of its immortality and perfect happiness; for whatever is excellent commands due reverence; at the same time that all fear of the might and anger of the Gods would be removed. For it is a matter of course that from an immortal and happy condition of being, anger and favour must be eliminated; and that, when these are removed, no fear of superior beings can haunt us. In order to establish this conviction, however, the mind inquires respecting the form and mode of life, and intellectual action and activity of the Deity.

18. 'On the question of form, intuition supplies some suggestions, and reason teaches us the rest; for all of us, of all nations, intuitively regard the form of the Gods as none other than human. What other form, in fact, has ever presented itself to anyone, either awake or asleep? But, without referring everything to intuitions, reason itself proclaims the same fact. For, as it seems to be consistent that the most excellent form of existence is also the most beautiful, either because it is happy, or because it is immortal; what symmetry of limbs, what outline of features, what face, what figure, can be more beautiful than the human? You indeed, Lucilius—for my friend Cotta adopts sometimes one and

sometimes the other theory—are in the habit, when imagining a sort of handicraft and divine workshop, of describing how adapted everything in the human form is, not only for use, but for beauty also. So that, if the human form surpasses those of all other living things, and the Deity is a living being, he is of course in that form which is of all the most beautiful. And since it is certain that Gods are perfectly happy, and that none can be happy without virtue, and virtue cannot exist without intelligence, and intelligence can exist in no other than human form, it must be admitted that the Gods are in human form. That form, however, is not a body, but an apparent body, and has not real but apparent blood.

19. 'Though this doctrine has been too ingeniously worked out, and too critically stated by Epicurus for everybody's comprehension, still, relying on your intelligence, I formulate it more concisely than the occasion demands. Epicurus, however, who not only took a mental view of abstruse and thoroughly mysterious subjects, but actually holds them—so to speak—in his hand, teaches us that the power and constitution of the Gods is such that it is perceived, in the first instance, not by the senses but by the mind; and not by any substance or enumeration, as are those objects which on account of their material nature he calls *Steremnia*, but by images made visible by resemblance and transference, and that, when an infinite view of closely resembling images proceeds from countless individual objects, and promanates to us; then the mind, attracted by its highest enjoyment to those images, and the attention fixed upon them, comprehends what is a happy and immortal condition of existence. But the supreme essence of infinity is fully entitled to long and diligent contemplation; for of this it must be understood that it is so constituted that all parts are equal and correspond to each other. This is what Epicurus calls *isonomia*, that is, equal distribution. From this, therefore, comes the inference that, if the number of mortal beings is so large, that of immortals cannot be less; and that, if the agencies of destruction are innumerable, conservative influences ought to be infinite. And in fact, Balbus, you are in the habit of asking us, what is the life of the Gods, and how time is spent by them? It is, of course, such that nothing more happy, more abundant in all enjoyments, can be imagined; for a God does nothing, is engaged in no occu-

pation, undertakes no work, finds pleasure in his own wisdom and virtue, and is certain of enjoyments at the same time perfect and everlasting.

20. 'Such a God we may truly call happy, but yours simply a drudge; for, if the world itself is God, what can be more destructive of repose than, without a moment's interval of rest, to be whirled round its axis with miraculous speed? For nothing can be happy but what is at rest; or, if there is in the world itself some God to rule and guide it, to maintain the revolutions of the stars and the successions of the seasons, to keep up the periodic changes and regularity of the universe, and, overlooking sea and land, to watch over the comforts and lives of men: surely, he must be engaged in troublesome and laborious occupations. We, on the contrary, identify a happy life with peace of mind and freedom from all duties; for he who taught us all the rest, has taught us this also, that the world is the work of nature, that there is no need of a workshop, and that the operation, which you say can be performed only by divine intelligence, is so easy that nature has created, is creating, and is likely to go on creating worlds without number. But, because you do not see how nature can effect this without some intelligent agency, like the tragic poets, when you cannot work out the conclusion of your argument, you resort to a God, whose assistance you would certainly not require if you could see that immeasurable and boundless extent of space in all directions, into which the mind, projecting and extending itself, travels so far and widely that it can find no limit where it may stop. In this infinity, then, of breadth and length and height, an infinite number of atoms is in motion, which, although space separates them, still unite together, and fastening on each other become inseparable; and from this union result those shapes and forms of objects which you say cannot be made without bellows and anvil. So that you have laid upon our necks an eternal master for us to regard with terror day and night. For, who would not be afraid of an all-foreseeing, all-designing, all-observant God, believing that all things belonged to himself, anxious and busy? Hence arises, in the first place, that inevitable destiny of yours which you call *eimarmene*. So that, whatever happens, you say that it proceeds from the eternal certainty and succession of causes; and what then is the value of that philosophy to

which everything seems to be predestined, as it would to old women, and very ignorant old women, too? The next doctrine is your *Mantiké*, which in Latin is named divination, by which, if we were to listen to you, we would be tainted with such superstition that we should revere sacrifice-inspectors, augurs, private fortune-tellers, public prophets, and interpreters of dreams. Freed from all these terrors by Epicurus, and set at liberty, we have no fear of those of whom we know that they neither make trouble for themselves nor inflict any upon others; and we dutifully and religiously worship the excellence and supremacy of nature. But, I fear that, carried away by my enthusiasm, I may have been too tedious; for it was difficult to break away from so attractive a subject when I began it, though I ought to have more regard to what I was to hear than to what I had to say.'

21. Then said Cotta, with his usual courtesy, 'And yet, Velleius, if you had not said something, you would have heard nothing whatever from me; for in general it does not so readily occur to me why any statement is true as why it is false: and this has been my case, as well on many former occasions, as just now, while listening to you. If you ask me what I think of the nature of Gods, I should probably have no answer to give. If you inquire whether I suppose it to be such as you have just now described it, I will say that nothing is farther from my belief. But, before I address myself to your argument, I will tell you what I think of yourself. For I think I have often heard that friend of yours, when he was confidently preferring you to all Romans, and comparing with you only a few of the Epicureans of Greece; but, as I knew that you were regarded by him with extraordinary affection, I thought that, through friendship, he was exaggerating. However, though I fear to praise a man to his face, I am of opinion that an obscure and difficult question has been treated by you clearly, not only with a richness of ideas, but with more elegance of language than your sect generally exhibit. When I was in Athens, I used constantly to hear Zeno, whom our friend Philo used to call the Corypheus of Epicureans, and, indeed, I believe it was by the advice of Philo himself, in order that I might judge how effectually those doctrines could be refuted, when I had heard how they were stated by the head of the Epicureans. He did not speak, then, in the usual style, but as you have

spoken, with clearness, dignity, and elegance; but, what used often to occur to me in his case, happened also, just now, while I was listening to you—a feeling of impatience that so powerful a mind—you will excuse me for saying it—should have conceived ideas so mean—not to say silly. Nor, indeed, have I, now, anything better of my own to produce; for, as I have just said, on almost all, and especially physical subjects, I can more readily speak negatively than affirmatively.

22. 'If you ask me what, in essence or attributes, is God, I will follow the example of Simonides, of whom, when King Hiero made this same inquiry, he demanded one day for reflection. When, on the next day, he put the same question to him, he asked for two days. When he repeatedly doubled the number of days, and Hiero, in amazement, inquired why he did so—"Because," he answered, "the longer I reflect on it, the more mysterious the subject seems to me." But I believe that Simonides—for he is said to have been, not only an interesting poet, but, in other respects, a wise and learned man—because many ingenious and fine-drawn theories occurred to his mind, was uncertain which of them was true, and despaired of truth altogether. But your master, Epicurus —for I would rather argue with him than with you—what does he say that is consistent, I will not say, with philosophy, but even with common sense?

'The first question in the inquiry respecting the nature of Gods is, whether or not Gods exist? It is difficult to answer negatively, I suppose, if the question is asked in a formal discussion, but in a conversation like this and a private meeting, easy enough. And, therefore, I, who am a priest, and believe that the formalities of national religion should be most reverently maintained, would like to be convinced of this fundamental fact that there are Gods, not merely as a matter of opinion, but as an actual certainty; for there are anomalies in the way; so that they sometimes appear to have no existence. But see how generously I am dealing with you : what you have in common with all other philosophers, I will not disturb, as, for instance, this very principle, for almost all men, and I myself, would like to believe that there are Gods, and accordingly I make no objection. The argument, however, which you adduce, I do not consider sufficiently valid.

23. 'You said, for instance, that the fact of such being

the belief of men of all nations and races, is a sufficient proof for an admission that there are Gods. But this is both intrinsically weak and erroneous: for, in the first place, how can you know the opinions of the nations? I believe, for my part, that there are some nations so barbarously savage that no perception of Gods exists among them. Well, then? Have not Diagoras, named 'the Godless,' and after him, Theodorus, abolished Gods altogether? For as to Protagoras of Abdera, the very greatest of the Sophists of that time, when at the beginning of an essay, he made this statement, "Of the Gods I cannot say either that they do or do not exist," he was, by order of the Athenian people, expelled from the city and territory, and his books publicly burnt. And, from that time, I believe that many men have become less ready to profess that opinion, when not even a doubt could escape punishment. What shall we say of persons guilty of sacrilege, blasphemy and perjury? As Lucilius says, "If Tubulus Lucius, or Lupus, or Carbo, or the son of Neptune" had ever believed in Gods, would he have been so forsworn or vicious? That argument of yours, therefore, is not so clearly demonstrated as it seems, for proving what you wish; but, as you use it in common with other philosophers, I will let it pass for the present; and would rather come to what is peculiar to yourselves.

'I admit the existence of Gods. Tell me, then, whence and where they are, what they are in person, in mind, in manner of life. These particulars I want to know. You employ for all purposes the supremacy and arbitrary power of atoms; of these you design and form whatever occurs first, as the saying is. But these, in the first place, have no existence; for there is no space not filled with matter; all space is occupied with it; so that there can be no vacuum, nothing indivisible.

24. 'What I am now repeating are maxims of the materialists: whether false or true I know not. But they are more probable than yours. For these are the absurdities of Democritus, and even of his predecessor, Leucippus: that some atoms are smooth and some rough; some round and others angular, and some curved and curled; that of these heaven and earth are made, by no force of nature, but a sort of accidental combination. This theory, Velleius, you have brought down to the present time; and one could more easily remove you from life altogether, than from that doc-

trine; because you decided that you ought to be an Epicurean before you learned it. So that you must either have accepted these absurdities, or, forfeit the name of your adopted philosophy.—What would you take for ceasing to be an Epicurean? Nothing whatever, you would say, for abandoning the means of a happy life and the truth. Is that, then, the truth? For I make no objection to your idea of a happy life; as you do not believe that it can be enjoyed even by a God, except by utterly stagnating in idleness. But, where is the truth? In countless worlds, I suppose, coming into existence and disappearing in every smallest measure of time; or is it in indivisible atoms forming all these glorious works without any controlling power of nature, and upon no system? But, I am forgetting the generosity with which I undertook, a while ago, to treat you, and am including too much. I will grant you, then, that all things consist of atoms. What has it to do with the question which relates to the nature of Gods? Suppose that they are formed of atoms: then they are not immortal; for whatever consists of atoms must have, at some time, had a beginning; if it had, there were no Gods before they began to be; and if birth is a condition of the Gods, so must death also be; as you were arguing a while ago respecting Plato's world.

'Where, then, is that happy and immortal being of yours, for by these two epithets you indicate God? But, when you attempt to realize the conception, you creep into the jungle; because you said that in God there was not a real but an apparent body; not real but apparent blood.

25. 'This is what you constantly do—when you assert something improbable and wish to escape censure, you bring forward something so utterly impossible, that it would have been better to concede the point in dispute than be so shamelessly obstinate. Epicurus, for instance, when he perceived that, if atoms were borne downwards by their own weight, we would be powerless in presence of their uniform and inevitable movement, discovered a mode of evading the difficulty, which had, of course, escaped the notice of Democritus. He says that an atom, in its directly downward course, diverges a little. To speak in this way is more scandalous than to be unable to prove what he wants. He adopts the same expedient against the logicians: for, as it is laid down by them, that in every dilemma, where "Yes" or "No" is required, one or the other must be true, fearing that,

if any such alternative were granted as this—either Epicurus will be alive to-morrow, or, he will not—one or the other would be inevitable, he denied altogether the necessity of the "Yes" or "No." What could be more stupid than this? Arcesilas used to assail Zeno, asserting that all the perceptions of sensation are illusions; while Zeno said that some, not all, are illusive. Epicurus, becoming afraid that, if any one perception were an illusion, none could be true, maintained that all our senses are reporters of truth. There was nothing in all this that was not ingenious. For he was ready to receive a heavier, in order to fend off a lighter blow. He does the same with reference to the nature of Gods: while he shrinks from an aggregate of atoms, lest death and dissolution should follow, he asserts that Gods have not a real but an apparent body, not real but apparent blood.

26. 'It seems strange that one sacrifice-inspector does not laugh when he sees another; and it is still more wonderful that you can refrain from laughing at each other. "It is not a real but an apparent body!" I could understand what this was like, if it was formed of wax or porcelain; but in the case of a God, what an apparent body or blood is, I cannot understand. Nor can you either, Velleius, though you won't confess it; for all those doctrines are repeated by you like lessons, which Epicurus dreamed when half asleep; since he boasted, as we find in his writings, that he had no teacher: and that I could very readily believe, even if he had not declared it, as I would believe the owner of a badly-built house, who boasted of not having an architect. For he has nothing that savours of the Academy; nothing of the Lycæum; nothing even of an elementary education. He might have heard Xenocrates—what a man that was! immortal Gods!—and there are some who think that he did hear him. He does not himself admit it; and there is none whom I am more inclined to believe. He says, that, in Samos, he heard one Pamphilus, a hearer of Plato—because, in his youth, he resided there with his father and brothers; as his father Neocles had come there as a colonist; but, as the farm did not produce sufficient income, I believe, he became a schoolmaster—but even him, though a pupil of Plato, he strangely held in contempt; such was his dread of the appearance of having been ever taught anything. He gives some attention to Nausiphanes, a pupil of Democritus,

upon whom he vents all sorts of insult, though he does not deny that he was a hearer of his. But, if he did not learn these doctrines of Democritus, what had he learned? What is there in the natural philosophy of Epicurus, that is not borrowed from Democritus? For, although he made some alterations, as, for instance, what I mentioned just now, about the diagonal course of atoms, he coincides in nearly everything—the atoms, the vacuum, the spectra, the infinity of space and of the number of worlds, their birth and death, and generally, all the elements of a system of nature.

'Now, what do you understand by this apparent body and apparent blood? For I not only admit, but am perfectly content with your superior knowledge of these doctrines. What is there that, when once it is stated, Velleius can understand, while Cotta can not? I can, therefore, understand what a body and what blood is, but an apparent body and blood, I am utterly unable to comprehend. You are not keeping a secret from me, as Pythagoras used from outsiders; nor are you purposely speaking darkly, like Heraclitus; but, between ourselves, even you do not understand it.

27. 'This, I believe, is what you insist upon: that the Gods have a sort of personality which has nothing actual in it, nothing material, nothing life-like, nothing tangible, and is unmixed, weightless, and transparent: we must say the same of it, then, as of the Venus of Cos: it is not a body, but the semblance of a body, nor is that mantling blush blended with whiteness real blood, but a semblance of it; so, in the God of Epicurus, there is no reality, but only its resemblance. Suppose that I am convinced—which cannot be even imagined—give me the features and forms of those shadowy Gods. There is, on this subject, no scarcity of arguments, by which you may prove, if so disposed, that the Gods are in human form—first, because it is so outlined and anticipated in our minds, that the human form suggests itself to man when he thinks of God. Secondly, because, as the divine essence excels all other things, its form also should be the most beautiful, and there is none that surpasses the human in beauty. You adduce a third argument; that intellect can have its dwelling in no other form. Now, let us begin by estimating the value of each separately; because you seem to me to seize, as if by some peculiar privilege, a conclusion by no means provable. Who, in fact, was ever so blind in observation as not to perceive that these illusive

shapes of men were attributed to Gods, either by some design of wise men, that they might more easily turn the minds of the ignorant from the errors of their lives to the worship of the Gods; or, by superstition: that there might be idols; and that when worshipping these they might believe that they were approaching the Gods themselves? On the other hand, poets, painters, and artizans encouraged those delusions; for it was not easy, when executing any work and portraying Gods, to continue in the reproduction of other forms. A further cause, perhaps, was that belief of the surpassing beauty of the human form to human eyes. But, do you not see, my natural philosopher, how plausibly persuasive nature is in self-commendation? Do you think that there is any beast on land, or in water, that is not attracted most by another of its own kind? If such were not the case, why should not a bull desire the society of a mare, and a horse that of a cow? Do you suppose that any eagle, or lion, or dolphin prefers any shape to its own? What wonder is it, then, if, on the same principle, nature has instructed man to consider nothing more beautiful than man, and that is the reason why we suppose that Gods resemble men?

28. How do you suppose it would be, if beasts were rational? Would they not severally attribute most excellence to their own species? But, in truth—for my part—for I will speak as I think—however I may be prejudiced in my own favour, I would not venture to say that I am more beautiful than that bull may have been that carried off Europa; for the question, at present, is not of our talent or our speeches, but of our personal appearance and form. But, if we choose to give scope to imagination and create composite forms, one would object to being like what that sea-born Triton is painted, riding upon swimming monsters attached to a human body. I am now involving myself in a difficulty: for the influence of nature is such, that no human being would like to resemble anything but man—as even one ant would resemble nothing but another—but, what sort of man? How few are beautiful! When I was in Athens, scarcely one of each class of youths could be found. I know why you smile; but the fact is so. Still further, to us who admire boys, under the sanction of ancient philosophers, even defects are sometimes pleasing. A mole on a boy pleases Alcæus; and yet, a mole is a bodily blemish. To him, however, it seemed a beauty. Q. Catulus, the father of our colleague and

friend here, admired your fellow-townsman Roscius, on whom this is his epigram—" I happened to be standing, greeting the rising dawn, when suddenly Roscius appeared—may I say it with your indulgence, ye natives of heaven?—the mortal seemed fairer than a God."

'To him he was fairer than a God; and yet he had, as he has to this day, most decidedly crooked eyes. What does it signify, if this very peculiarity seemed to him piquant and fascinating? I come back to the Gods.

29. 'Are we to suppose that any of them are, if not quite so goggle-eyed, at least pink-eyed? that any of them have warts? that any are flat-nosed, flap-eared, beetle-browed, large-headed—defects common among us? Are all features faultless in them? Let that be granted you. Have they all one style of face? Because, if they have several, one must be more beautiful than another: therefore, some God must be less than perfectly beautiful. If their appearance is all the same, the Academy must be popular in heaven; for, if there is no difference between one God and another, there can be no identification among the Gods, no perception. Well, then? If this theory also, Velleius, is totally false, that when thinking of Gods, no form but human occurs to us, can you still maintain such absurdities? To us, perhaps, that idea does occur, as you say; because from our childhood we have known Jupiter, Juno, Minerva, Neptune, Vulcan, Apollo, and the rest of the Gods, by that personal appearance which painters and sculptors fancied; and not by that only, but their accessories, age and dress. But it is not so with Syrians and Egyptians, and foreigners generally; for you will find that their convictions respecting certain beasts are stronger than ours respecting the most hallowed temples and statues of the Gods. We know, for instance, that many shrines have been robbed and statues of Gods removed from the most holy places of our people; but it has never been heard, even by hearsay, that a crocodile, or an ibis, or a cat had been insulted by an Egyptian. What do you think, then? Don't you suppose that Apis, the consecrated bull of the Egyptians, is regarded by them as a God? As much so, without doubt, as your goddess Sospita is by you, though you never see her, even in a dream, but with her goat-skin, lance, shield, and broad-soled shoes. But neither the Argive nor the Roman Juno is so habited; so that the Argives and Lanuvini recognise different forms of Juno; and, in fact, our

idea of Jupiter Capitolinus is different from the African's conception of Jupiter Hammon.

30. 'Is it not, then, a shame for a natural philosopher—that is, a student and explorer of nature—to look for evidence of truth from minds influenced by habit? For, on that principle, it will be possible to describe Jupiter as always bearded, Apollo ever beardless, Minerva's eyes blue, and Neptune's green. We admire, as a matter of course, the Athenian Vulcan which Alcamenes wrought, in which, standing and draped as it is, there appears a slight lameness not amounting to deformity. We shall have a lame God, then; as such is the tradition respecting Vulcan.

'Well, now; let us assume that there are Gods bearing those names by which they are known to us. But, in the first place, the names of Gods are as many as there are human languages; because, Vulcan is not the same in Italy as in Africa or Spain; as you, wherever you go, are still Velleius. Secondly, the number of names is not large, even in the pontifical books, while the number of Gods is incalculable. Are they, then, without names? That is just what you must admit; for, of what use is it that the names are many, when their appearance is uniform? How creditable would it be, Velleius, to confess your ignorance of what you knew not, instead of sickening and disgusting yourself by talking such nonsense! Do you suppose that God resembles you or me? You certainly do not. Well, then, am I to call the sun, or moon, or sky a God?—and happy too?—enjoying what pleasures?—and wise? How can wisdom exist in a shapeless mass of that sort? Such are your doctrines. If, then, he exists neither in human form—as I have shown—nor in any other resembling it, as you are convinced, why do you hesitate to deny the existence of Gods? You have not the courage. That certainly is prudent. Though, in this particular, it is not the people that you fear, but the Gods themselves. I know Epicureans who keep account of all statues; although I perceive that to some of them Epicurus appears to have ostensibly spared the Gods and practically abolished them; and, accordingly, in those select and concise opinions of his, which you call "the orthodox maxims," the first dogma, I believe, is this—"That which is happy and immortal neither takes trouble nor gives it to anyone."

31. 'In this doctrine, stated as it is, there are some who believe that he did purposely what he did simply through

ignorance of language. They judge unjustly a man by no means crafty; for it is uncertain whether he means that anything is happy and immortal; or, that whatever is happy is immortal. They don't see that here he speaks ambiguously, but that, in many other places, both he and Metrodorus speak as plainly as you did just now. He, however, believes that there are Gods, and I have never seen any man who stood in greater terror of that which he says should not be feared—I mean death and the Gods. Considerations by which ordinary men are not influenced, by these he proclaims that the minds of all mortals are dismayed. So many thousands commit robbery, with death in prospect; others plunder as many temples as they can. Fear of death, I suppose, deters the former; or religion the latter!

'But, since you don't venture—for I am now speaking to Epicurus himself—to deny the existence of Gods, what is there to prevent you from regarding the sun, or the world, or some eternal intelligence in the character of Gods? I have never seen, you say, a soul possessing reason and intellect in any other than human form. Well? Have you ever seen anything like the sun, or the moon, or the five planets? The sun, confining his motion to the utmost extent of one circle, completes his circuit in a year. This revolution of his, the moon, illumined by his light, accomplishes in the space of a month; while the five planets, keeping the same plane, some nearer to, some farther from the earth, complete the same course in different periods. Have you ever seen anything like that, Epicurus? Let there be, then, no sun, no moon, no planets, since nothing can exist but what we have handled and seen!

'Well? Have you ever seen God himself? Why do you believe that he exists? Let us, then, annihilate everything that either history or a new theory suggests to us! Thus it is that the dwellers inland cannot believe in the existence of the sea. What narrowness of mind this is! It is just as if you had been born in Seriphos, and had never left the island, where you had constantly seen hares and foxes. You would not believe the existence of lions and panthers, if they were described to you. But, if anyone were to tell you of an elephant, you would suppose that you were actually the victim of a joke.

32. 'And in fact you, Velleius, not on your own method, but that of the logicians, have supported your doctrine by a

form of argument of which your sect are totally ignorant. You have assumed that the Gods are happy—we grant it—and that none can be happy without virtue; that also we admit, and readily too—and that virtue can have no existence without reason. On that point also we must agree. You add, that reason can exist only in human form. Who do you suppose will grant you that? If it were so, why need you have come step by step to that point? You might have taken it as your right. But, what is this step-by-step argument? I perceive that you have come, by steps, from happiness to virtue; and from virtue to reason; but, from reason to the human form how do you come? That transition is like falling down a cliff instead of walking down. Nor, indeed, can I understand why Epicurus chose to say that Gods are like men, rather than that men are like Gods. You will ask, what is the difference? for, if this is like that, that is like this. I know that. But, what I mean is this—that it was not from men that their form passed to the Gods; because the Gods existed always, and were never born, as they are to be immortal; but men are born, and therefore the human form, which the Gods bear, existed before men. It is not, therefore, their form that should be called human, but ours divine. This, however, may be as you please. This I want to know; how came such good luck—for you believe that nothing in the creation resulted from design. Still, how came that fortunate accident—that happy combination of atoms—that men should be, all at once, born in the form of Gods? Are we to suppose that germs of Gods fell from heaven to earth, and that men, accordingly, grew in the shape of their parents? I wish you would tell me. I would be glad to acknowledge a kinship with the Gods. You make no such statement, but that it happened by chance that we are like the Gods. Now, arguments to refute this are to be sought, and I wish I could discover the truth as easily as I can refute mistakes.

33. 'You have counted up, with a long memory and full detail—so that I was agreeably surprised by so much learning in a Roman—the views of all the philosophers, down from Thales of Miletus, respecting the nature of Gods. Do all these appear to you to be mistaken, who pronounced it possible for a God to be formed without hands and feet? Does not even this consideration influence you—the usefulness and convenience of limbs in the human body—to decide that Gods have no need of human limbs? For, what need is

there of feet without motion? What need of hands, if there is nothing to hold? What need of the rest of the whole system of bodily organs, in which there is nothing useless, nothing accidental, nothing superfluous?—so that no art can imitate the ingenuity of nature—shall a God, then, have a tongue and never speak? teeth, palate, and jaws for no useful purpose; and the generative organs which nature has attached to the body—shall a God have these superfluously? and not only the external but the internal organs —heart, lungs, liver, and the rest—for, apart from their uses, what beauty have these? since you will attribute all these to a God, for sake of mere symmetry. Was it in reliance on these dreams that not only Epicurus and Metrodorus and Hemarchus argued against Pythagoras and Plato and Empedocles, but even the little courtesan, Leontium, had the impudence to write against Theophrastus? Her style, indeed, is learned and Attic; but still—such was the freedom of the garden of Epicurus. And yet, you are in the habit of complaining! Zeno, indeed, used to scold. Why should I speak of Albucius! For nothing can be more polished and courteous than Phædrus. But the old man used to lose his temper, if I said anything too severe; though Epicurus worried Aristotle most insultingly, and most shamefully abused Socrates' friend Phædrus; wrote whole volumes of invective against Timocrates, the brother of your friend Metrodorus; was ungrateful to Democritus himself, whom he followed, and treated so badly his own teacher, Nausiphanes, from whom he certainly learned something.

34. 'Zeno, indeed, used to wound with his insults not only the men of that time, Apollodorus, Syllus and all the rest, but Socrates himself, the father of philosophy, he used to call—using a Latin phrase—an Attic buffoon; and Chrysippus he never called anything but Chrysippa. Even you, too, just a while ago, when enumerating—so to speak—a senate of philosophers, described first-rate men as fools, blunderers, and lunatics; although, if none of them perceived the truth respecting the nature of Gods, there is reason to fear that there is no such thing at all; for what you assert is all imaginary, and scarcely worthy of the invention of old women. You do not perceive how much you must assume, if you prevail on us to grant that the form of men and Gods is the same; for all the same decoration and care of the body must be employed by God as by man—walking, running, reclining, stooping,

sitting, the use of the hands, and, in short, the same familiar and public speaking. As to your description of Gods as male and female—you know the inference. In fact, I cannot adequately express my amazement how that master of yours arrived at such opinions. But, you are never tired of insisting upon the vindication of this doctrine, that a God must be happy and immortal. And what prevents him from being happy, if he is not a biped; or, why is it that such happiness or beatitude—whichever it is, though both terms are harsh and require softening by use—cannot be attributed to the sun, or to this world, or to some immortal intelligence apart from material form and bodily limbs? You can say nothing but this—"I have never seen a sun or world happy." Well? Have you ever seen any world but this? You will say "No." Why, then, have you presumed to say that there are not merely six hundred thousand worlds, but numbers incalculable? Reason teaches it. Will not reason, then, teach you this, that—when the most perfect nature is in question, and that happy and immortal, which are exclusively divine attributes—as we are surpassed by that nature in immortality, we are also surpassed in perfection of mind; and, if of mind, of body also? Why, then, when inferior in other respects, are we equal in form? for, in point of resemblance, human nature would approach the Deity morally, more nearly than physically.

35. 'Can anything so childish be asserted—to follow up the same topic still further—as to deny the existence of those species of animals which are produced in the Red Sea, or in India? And yet, not even the most inquisitive men can by research even hear of as many as live on land, in the sea, in marshes and rivers; and we are to deny the existence of all these, because we have never seen them! But how little the actual resemblance, which specially takes your fancy, has to do with the question! Why, is not a dog like a wolf? And, as Ennius says: "How closely the ape, most hideous of animals, resembles us!" But in both cases, the instincts are different. There is no beast more sagacious than the elephant. And in size what other exceeds it? I am speaking of beasts. Well? Even among men, are there not different dispositions in the closest personal resemblances, and personal differences with the most similar dispositions? In fact, Velleius, if we once adopt this form of argument, consider to what conclusion it may proceed. For you

assumed that, except in human form, reason cannot exist. Another man may assume that it can have no place, except in one who has been born—except one who has attained maturity —one who has been educated—one who consists of mind and a frail and feeble body—finally, except in a human and mortal being. But, if you object in all these cases, why should form alone present a difficulty? For, under all those conditions which I have suggested, you saw that reason and intellect are human attributes; and, if all these are excluded, you still profess to recognise a God, if only the visible form remains. This is not deliberation, but taking chance for what you are to say. But perhaps you do not consider even this, that not only in the case of a man, but even of a tree, whatever is superfluous or useless, is objectionable. What a nuisance it is to have one finger too many! Why so? Because the five do not require another either for ornament or use. But your God is uselessly encumbered not only with one finger, but with head, neck, shoulders, sides, stomach, back, hams, hands, feet and legs: if for the purpose of being immortal, what have limbs to do with such a life? These are more to the purpose—brain, heart, lungs, and liver—for they are so many seats of life: the formation of the face has nothing to do with permanence of life.

36. 'And yet, you would denounce those who, when they looked upon the world itself and its divisions—heaven, earth and sea, and their embellishments—sun, moon and planets; and observed the growth and changes and revolutions of the seasons, inferred from these glorious and perfect works that there must be some excellent and perfect essence that created, set in motion, kept in order and guided all this. And, even if these men are astray in their hypothesis, still I see what they mean. As for you—what great and matchless work do you know, executed apparently by divine intelligence, from which you infer the existence of Gods. "I had," you say, "an intuitive perception of a God implanted in my mind." Was it of a bearded Jupiter, and a helmeted Minerva: do you believe that they are like these? How much better the ignorant multitude understand this subject! for they attribute to Gods not only human limbs, but the use of them. They give them, for instance, a bow and arrows, a lance, a shield, a hunting-spear, the lightning-bolt, and though there be some divine action which they cannot see, still they cannot imagine a totally inactive God. Even the Egyptians, who incur our

ridicule, never deified any animal except for some benefit which they derived from it: as the ibis destroys a large number of serpents, being a tall bird, with stiff legs and a long horny beak; it defends Egypt from pestilence, by killing and devouring the flying snakes brought from the Libyan desert by the south wind; whence it happens that they neither poison anyone while living with their fangs, nor when dead by their smell. I can mention, also, the usefulness of the ichneumon, the crocodile, and the cat; but I won't be tedious. I will, however, conclude by saying that animals are deified by foreigners for benefits received; while from your Gods not only is no benefit apparent, but none has ever been realized at all.

37. 'The Deity, he says, takes no trouble. In fact, Epicurus, like pampered youths, thinks nothing better than a vacation. But, even those youths, during their idleness, amuse themselves with some athletic exercise; but we suppose that a God, exempt from work, so stagnates in idleness, that, if he moved, we fear that he cannot be happy! This declaration not only deprives the Gods of motion and divine activity, but makes men also inactive, since, if he does anything, not even a God can be happy. But, suppose, as you maintain, that God is in the form and likeness of man; where is his home, his residence, his locality; finally, what is his mode of life? In what respects—as you maintain—is he happy? For, whoever means to be happy, must use and enjoy his own advantages; because even those natural objects that are inanimate, have their several permanent places; so that the earth occupies the lowest, the water overflows it; a higher region is assigned to the air, and the highest to fiery bodies. Of the lower animals, again, some belong to the land, some to the water; and some are amphibious, living in both elements: there are some also that are supposed to be produced in fire, and are often seen flying about in blazing furnaces. I want to know, therefore, in the first place, where your Deity dwells: secondly, what motive withdraws him from his place — if he ever does move — and lastly — as it belongs to all living things to desire something suited to their nature—what does the Deity desire; for what purpose, in fact, does he employ his will and reason; and finally, in what way he is happy, and how immortal? Whichever of these questions you touch, is a sore point. An argument so badly stated cannot work out a conclusion. For this is what you

said: that the perception of a Deity is attained by reflection, and not by material sensation; that there is no substance in it; that it does not continue uniform in number; and that its aspect is such that it is made visible only by resemblance and transferrence; and that from innumerable atoms, an accession of similar bodies is never deficient; and hence it comes that our minds, bent on all this, regard that essence as happy and immortal.

38. 'In the name of the Gods, of whom we are speaking, what can be the meaning of this? Because, if they are effective only for mental perception, and have no substance or tangibility, what difference does it make whether we imagine a Hippocentaur or a God? For every such mental representation all other philosophers call an illusion; but you describe it as the arrival and entrance of ideas into the mind. So that, as when I fancy that I see Tib. Gracchus speaking in the Capitol, and handing round the ballot-box against M. Octavius, I call that mental impulse an illusion: you say, on the contrary, that the phantoms of Gracchus and Octavius are permanent, which on their arrival at the Capitol are brought back to my mind, and that the effect is the same in the case of a God, by whose frequent presence our minds are so influenced that they are believed to be happy and immortal. Suppose that there really are phantoms to which the mind is sensitive, it is merely an optical illusion that is present; and is there any reason why it should be happy, or, why it should be immortal? But, what are those phantoms of yours, or whence? This extravagance originates altogether with Democritus; but he is censured by many, and you can find no escape, and the whole system is unstable and lame. For, what can be less probable than that phantoms of Homer, Archilochus, Romulus, Numa, Pythagoras, and Plato, should all be present with me, and not in the shape in which they lived? How, then, are they identified? and whose are the phantoms? Aristotle tells us that Orpheus, as a poet, never existed, and the poem known as "Orphic" was really the work of Cercops, a Pythagorean. Still, Orpheus, that is, his phantom, as you will have it, often comes into my mind. How is it that I have one impression, and you another, of the same person?—that there are ideas of things that never existed at all, and could not exist, of Scylla, of the Chimæra, for instance? How, of persons, and places, and those cities which we have never seen? How is

it that, as soon as I please, a phantom is present, and they come to me uncalled, even when asleep? The whole system, Velleius, is nonsensical!

39. 'You, however, impose phantoms not merely on the eye, but on the mind. Such is the license of twaddle! And how extravagantly! There comes a transferrence of constantly emanating phantoms, so that of the many one is visible! I would be ashamed to say that I don't understand it, if you understood it yourselves, who maintain that doctrine. How can you prove that phantoms are constantly coming? or, if constantly, how are they eternal? Atoms innumerable, you say, keep up the supply; but, then, will that cause them all to be everlasting also? You resort to your equilibration—for so, if you please, let us translate *isonomia*—and say that, as there is a mortal, there must also be an immortal nature. On that principle, as there are mortal men, there should be some immortal; and as there are products of earth, there should be also of water. Because there are destructive, there should be also conservative agencies. Suppose that there are, what have they to conserve? Not such Gods as these, I think. How does all this visionary world arise from individual atoms? For, even if they had any existence—which they have not—they might, perhaps, displace and come into collision with each other, but they could never constitute, or shape anything, or impart colour or life. You can, therefore, by no means, make your God immortal.

40. 'Now let us consider the question of happiness. Without virtue certainly it can never be; but virtue is active, and your God totally inactive, and therefore, destitute of virtue, and consequently, not even happy. What, then, is his mode of life? Abundance of good, you say, without any alloy of evil. Of what good, then? Pleasures connected with the body, I suppose; for you recognise no mental enjoyment but what proceeds from, and reacts upon the body. I do not suppose that you, Velleius, are like other Epicureans, who are ashamed of some sayings of Epicurus, in which he confesses that he cannot even imagine any good, distinct from luxurious and sensual pleasures, all which he enumerates by name, without a blush. What food, then, or what drink, what variety of music or flowers; what sensations of touch, what perfumes, will you supply to the Gods, to steep them in enjoyment? The poets, however, provide them with nectar and ambrosia for food, and Juventas or Ganymede as cup-

bearer. But, what will you do for them, Epicurus? for I cannot see whence your God is to obtain these things, or, how he is to enjoy them. Human nature, then, is richer than the divine in the elements of a happy life; because it enjoys several kinds of pleasure. But you speak of these as smaller pleasures, by which a sort of titillation — a term borrowed from Epicurus—is applied to the senses. How far are you carrying the jest? Even our friend Philo could not bear to see Epicurus rejecting luxurious and sensuous pleasures, for, with his perfect memory, he used to repeat many opinions of Epicurus in the actual words in which they were written; and, of Metrodorus, who was a brother philosopher of Epicurus, he used to quote still more shameless doctrines; for, Metrodorus charges his own brother, Timocrates, with hesitating to measure, by the appetite, all that contributes to a happy life, and says so, not once, but repeatedly. I see that you acknowledge it—of course you know it—I would produce the books, if you denied it. And I am not, now, objecting to the estimation of everything by sensual enjoyment—that is a separate question—but showing you that your Gods are incapable of enjoyment, and therefore, on your estimate, not even happy.

41. 'But they are exempt from suffering. Is that sufficient for that perfectly happy life abounding in good? He is constantly contemplating his own happiness, they say, for he has nothing else to think of. Imagine, then, and set before your eyes a God doing nothing else through all eternity than thinking, "I'm all right, I'm happy!" And yet, I don't see how that happy God can escape the apprehension that he may die; since he is, without any intermission, pelted and disquieted by the continual impact of atoms, while phantoms are perpetually issuing from him; so that your God is neither happy nor immortal. But Epicurus actually wrote essays upon sanctity and devotion to the Gods; and in these how does he speak? In such a style that you might say that you were listening to Coruncanius, or Scævola, the high priests; not to the man who abolished all religion whatever, and overthrew the temples and altars of the immortal Gods, not by physical force, as Xerxes did, but by argument. Why should you say that the Gods should be worshipped by men, when the Gods not only have no regard for men, but care for nothing whatever, and do nothing? But, then, their nature is so transcendent and excellent, that it must of itself induce

a wise man to worship it. Can there be anything excellent in that nature which, enjoying merely its own gratification, is never likely to do, never does or has done anything? Still more, what devotion is due to one from whom you have received nothing? or, what in any sense can be due to him who has no claim? Because devotion is justice toward the Gods; and between them and us what obligations can exist, when man has no fellowship with God? Sanctity is knowledge of the worship of the Gods; and why they are to be worshipped I cannot understand, as no benefit is either received or expected from them.

42. 'What reason is there, again, why we should revere the Gods in admiration of that nature in which we see nothing uncommon; because the freedom from superstition, of which you are in the habit of boasting, is easy when you deprive the Gods of all power. Unless it may be that you suppose Diagoras or Theodorus, who denied the existence of Gods altogether, capable of being superstitious. I don't believe it even of Protagoras, who was not free either to affirm or deny that there are Gods. For their opinions abolish not only universal superstition, which involves an idle fear of the Gods, but religion also, which consists in dutiful worship of the Gods. Well, they who say that the whole doctrine respecting immortal Gods was invented by wise men, under a political motive, in order that religion might bring to their duty those whom reason could not—have not they totally abolished all religion? What religion has Prodicus of Cos left in existence, who said that those objects which benefited human life have been included in the number of Gods? Well, are not they destitute of all religion who teach that brave and distinguished and powerful men have, after death, raised themselves to the Gods; and that these are the same that we are accustomed to pray to and worship? This theory has been illustrated most fully by Enemerus, whom our countryman Ennius has translated and followed more than all others. But, by Enemerus the death and burial of Gods are described. Does he seem to have established religion, or, to have abolished it altogether? I pass by Eleusis the holy and venerable, "where the most distant nations of the world are initiated." I pass by Samothracia, and the ceremonies that "in Lemnos are celebrated in the gloom of the midnight visit, hidden by the forest jungle," for when these are exposed and brought to the test of reason, it is the nature of

material objects rather than that of the Gods that is made known.

43. 'To me, in fact, Democritus, one among the first of great men, from whose fountains Epicurus watered his little garden, seems to be uncertain respecting the nature of Gods; for, at one time, he signifies his belief that phantoms invested with divinity exist in the universal creation; at another, that elements of intellect, which are in the same universe, are Gods; at another, living phantoms which are generally friendly or hostile to us; and again, some gigantic phantoms, so large that they surround the whole world externally—all which is more worthy of the country of Democritus than of himself. For, who can grasp those phantoms in his imagination? Who can contemplate them? Who can consider them entitled to worship or religious respect? Epicurus, however, uprooted religion from men's minds when he deprived the Gods of power to help and gratitude. He destroys that which is the special attribute of the highest and most excellent nature; for, what is better or more excellent than kindness and beneficence? And, when you would have a God destitute of this, you mean that nobody—neither God nor man—is dear to God; nobody loved, nobody preferred by him; and so it happens that not only are men neglected by Gods, but Gods mutually by each other.

44. 'How much better the Stoics teach, who are censured by you! They believe that wise men are the friends of other wise men, though they may be strangers; for nothing is more amiable than virtue, and whoever can attain that, wherever he is, will be valued by us. But you—what mischief you do when you make kindness and benevolence depend on helplessness! Because, though I should say nothing of the power and character of the Gods, do you suppose that men would not be benevolent and generous unless they were mutually dependent? Is there no natural affection between good men? The mere name of love (*amor*) is dear, and from that the term friendship (*amicitia*) is derived. But, if we estimate this by our own advantage, not by that of our friend, it will be not friendship, but a mere barter of personal benefits. Upon this principle, fields and crops and flocks of sheep are loved, because profit is derived from them; but between men affection and friendship are disinterested: how much more so, then, that of the Gods, who, wanting nothing, love each other and provide for men! Because, if it is not

so, why do we worship and pray to the Gods? Why do priests preside over sacrifices, and augurs over auspices? What can we desire from the immortal Gods? Why make vows? Still there is an essay on piety by Epicurus. We are mocked by a man who is not so much witty as he abuses the freedom of literary license: for, what piety can there be if the Gods take no interest in human affairs? and what living being can there be that cares for nothing? To all appearance, therefore, that is more true which our common friend Poseidonius argued in his fifth book on the nature of Gods. That it is the opinion of Epicurus that there are no Gods, and that, what he said about them, he said for the purpose of escaping censure, because he would not be so stupid as to represent a God in human form, merely in outline and not substantially, furnished with all the human limbs, but not the smallest use for any of them; a shadowy and transparent being, caring for nothing whatever and doing nothing. In the first place, there could be no such being; and perceiving that, Epicurus, while virtually abolishing Gods, ostensibly left them in existence. Secondly, even if it is ever so certain that there is a God so constituted that he can be influenced by no gratitude, by no human affection, farewell to him! For why should I say, "May he be propitious," because propitious to any he cannot be; since, as you say, all gratitude and kindness consist in mutual dependence.'

NOTES TO BOOK I.

CH. 18. *Quoniam Deos beatissimos esse constat.* This often-quoted sorites —or chain-syllogism—which, in logical form, would stand thus—The Gods are happy: the happy are virtuous: the virtuous are intellectual: the intellectual can be only in human form: therefore, the Gods are in human form—exhibits in the last premise the defect known to logicians as *fallacia accidentis;* because fully-developed intellect is exclusively limited to the human form, only so far as our knowledge and experience extend. We cannot assert that there are not, in other and higher worlds, beings of a much higher order of intellect than any of ourselves; nor, by analogy, can we deny that there are, elsewhere, forms of physical organization as far superior to ours as we are to quadrupeds. This, however, is not the special fault in the argument against which Cotta directs his refutation. He objects to the anthropomorphic theory upon many grounds; and several of these objections, impartially estimated, do certainly seem disingenuous and sophistical. For instance, to that stated in ch. 29, it may be replied that the occasional deformity of human beings is no argument against the uniform beauty of Gods; and, that it is not a valid *reductio ad impossibile* to urge that, if all Gods are specimens of anthropoid beauty, it must be impossible to distinguish one from another, because it is not so in the case of men or women; and, as against the same hypothesis, it is totally irrelevant to ask if any of them are deformed.

Again, the objection in ch. 30 may be answered by observing that difference of names in different languages cannot prove or disprove anything. It may as well be said that no man named Louis was ever King of France, because that name is, in Latin, Ludovicus, and in Welsh, Llewellyn; and, if Velleius had been as long and as widely known as Vulcan, he would certainly have had as many names.

In answer to the trifling objection—*non ergo*, etc.—in ch. 32, we may say that, if man was made in the likeness of God—or, the Gods—then his form must be the same as ours, and we have no other mode of describing it than that used by Epicurus: and to that stated in ch. 34—*formâ pares*, etc.—we may reply that the most physically perfect human beings are sometimes deficient in intellect, while the highest mental faculties occasionally dwell even in deformed bodies; and that there is no analogy; except, perhaps, in the head.

Ch. 25. *Tanquam corpus*, etc. What Epicurus meant and Cotta found it so impossible to understand, seems to be this—that, as our bodies are suited to the state of transition in which we exist, those of the Gods should be equally adapted to conditions of eternity; differently constituted, and resembling ours only in external appearance—such bodies, in fact, as St. Paul promises that we shall, ourselves, inhabit in the future life; and, accordingly, we find the Greek poets assigning to the Gods a totally different sort of food and different blood from ours.

Ch. 34. The argument running through this chapter—*argumentum ad ignorantiam*—has always been one of the most plausible and popular of sophisms: because, though obviously false, it may, in syllogistic form, be perfect in mood and figure. We are required to believe, or admit, a given statement, no matter how intrinsically improbable, because we know nothing that can directly disprove it. Here, for instance, the Epicurean is called upon to admit the falsehood of the anthropomorphic theory, because he has never actually seen a God, and cannot prove by actual demonstration that God may not exist in any other, or even in no visible form. He does not, of course, doubt the existence of animals which he has never seen, because he believes the recorded testimony of other men who have seen them, and could, himself, see them, if sufficiently near. But this is a false analogy, being negative on one side and positive on the other; and further, as the Stoic admits that, in some moral and intellectual attributes, we approach the Deity, it is the more probable that he resembles us in form also. It is by this argument *ad ignorantiam* that miraculous and supernatural events are generally proved; because, being unable to deny that all things are possible to omnipotence, we are required to concede the truth of any arbitrary assertion.

Ch. 37. The objection urged here is scarcely a fair statement of the theory of Epicurus; because all that he really cared to dispute was the interference of the Gods with physical laws. He represents them, simply, as too much absorbed in their own placid enjoyments to trouble themselves with creation and providence. As described by him, they would be analogous to an exclusively select aristocratic circle of human beings, pursuing their own pleasures and cultivating their own accomplishments, ignorant and heedless of the concerns of the lower strata of society all round them, but not, for that cause, necessarily inactive. Some theologians, indeed, have in all ages assumed that this planet and its inhabitants are, if not the whole creation, the most important portion of it, and entitled, accordingly, to the larger share of divine supervision.

Ch. 38. *Quid interest utrum*, etc. The objection involved in this question seems to be founded on the hypothesis that nothing can exist but matter. In that case Cotta is only elaborately refuting what Epicurus never asserted. There is no analogy between a centaur, which is nothing, if not material, and a God, who may be both spiritual and material or spiritual only. When he asks how the originals of the *imagines*, or ideas, can be identified, the obvious answer is—By the resemblance, real or imaginary, without which they could not be *imagines*. At the same time, it was never claimed for the Greek statues that they were portraits, or anything more than so many realized conceptions of beauty more or less ideal. That different persons, fortunately, have different ideas of the same object is merely because they are different persons. We can have ideas of composite emblematic figures, which never had any living existence, because the artists who created them had the faculty of imagination—*i.e.*, of forming new combinations of existing impressions; and we recall past impressions, because we have the faculty of recollection, without which we could have no accumulated knowledge. If we could have ideas only of those objects which are within the range of our material senses, our knowledge would be very limited : we should have no memory ; and yet this seems to be the alternative proposed by the Stoics. But all these questions relate but very indirectly to the Epicurean theory of Gods.

In this association, there is some difficulty in adequately translating *imago*. The term *image* or *idea*, in the metaphysical sense, would express it ; but would probably be misunderstood by most readers. I have used the term *phantom*, as being, perhaps, the least likely to mislead.

Of the ancient philosophers, the Peripatetics were those, principally, who believed that images of external objects pass from them, through the senses, into the mind, and that external objects are not themselves perceived, but only these images. This theory, of which the latter half was adopted by Des Cartes, was altogether rejected by Hobbes, Locke, and Reid.

BOOK II.

1. WHEN Cotta had so spoken, then said Velleius: 'I have certainly been rash in attempting to enter the lists with one who is, at the same time, an Academic and an orator. For, I would have feared neither an ineloquent Academic, nor an orator, however fluent, without that philosophy; because I am disconcerted neither by a torrent of empty words, nor by ingenuity of thought if there is a dearth of words. You, Cotta, however, have been strong in both qualities: you wanted only an audience and a jury of umpires—but of that hereafter—at present, let us hear Lucilius, if convenient to him.' Then said Balbus, 'For my part, I would rather hear Cotta still, provided that he could introduce to us the true Gods with the same eloquence wherewith he has abolished the false; for it is the duty of a philosopher and priest, and of Cotta, to have, not like the Academics, an unsteady and wavering belief, but, as our school has, fixed and definite; because against Epicurus quite enough has been said. But I am anxious, Cotta, to hear what your own opinion is.' 'Have you forgotten,' said he, 'what I said at first,—that I can more easily tell, especially on such questions, what I do not, than what I do believe? So that, even if I had any certainty, I would still prefer to hear you in your turn, after having said so much myself.' Then said Balbus, 'I will gratify you, and treat the subject as briefly as I can; because, by the refutation of the errors of the Epicureans a long discussion is cut off my argument. In short, our school divide the whole of this question respecting immortal Gods into four heads. First, they teach that there are Gods. Secondly, the character of their attributes. Next, that the world is governed by them; lastly, that they take an interest in human affairs. Let us, however, in this conversation, take up the first two: the third and fourth, which are larger questions, may be postponed, I think, to another occasion.' 'By no means,' said Cotta; 'for we are at leisure, and, at

the same time, discussing subjects which should take precedence even of business.'

2. Then said Lucilius: 'The first proposition seems not even to require discussion. For, what can be so plain and evident, when we look up to the heavens and study celestial objects, as the presence of some power of transcendent intellect by which all these are controlled? Because, if it were not so, how could Ennius have said, with universal acquiescence, "Behold, this empyrean expanse which all men address as Jove,"—the same, in fact, who is both Jupiter and the ruler of the world, and, as Ennius also says: "father of Gods and men," and a living and all-powerful God? And, whoever doubts this—I cannot well see why he does not also doubt whether or not the sun exists. How is this fact more evident than that? And unless we held this as a known and understood fact, the belief would not remain so fixed, nor be strengthened by length of time, nor could it have grown old with the centuries and generations of men. For, we see that other beliefs, imaginary and idle, have faded away. Who, for instance, believes that a Centaur or a Chimæra ever lived? or, what old woman can be found so stupid as to fear those monsters of the lower world that were once matters of belief? Time, in fact, blots out the fictions of creeds, and establishes the verdicts of nature; and accordingly, both in our own community and others, the worship of the Gods and the sanctity of religion are becoming, every day, wider and better. And this happens not without cause or by chance, but because the Gods often reveal their actual presence; as, at the Lake Regillus, in the Latin war, when the Dictator A. Postumius met Mamilius of Tusculum in the field, Castor and Pollux were seen fighting on our side on horseback; and at a later date, the same sons of Tyndarus announced the defeat of Perses. Because P. Vatinius, grandfather of the present young man, when two youths on white horses told him, on his way by night from the præfecture of Reate to Rome, that King Perses was that day made a prisoner, reported it to the Senate; and at first, on the charge of having spoken lightly respecting the Republic, was thrown into prison; and afterwards, on the arrival of despatches from Paullus, when the dates were found to coincide, was rewarded by the Senate with an estate and a patent of exemption. Still further, when the Locri had defeated the Crotoniats in a great battle on the river Sagra,

it is recorded that the battle was reported, the same day, at the Olympic games. The frequent sound of the voices of the Fawns, the frequent appearance of the forms of Gods, have forced every one not stupid or impious to confess that the Gods are living.

3. 'But, what else do predictions and presentiments of coming events imply, than that the events are shown and indicated, foreboded and foretold to men? And hence figurations, indications, portents and prodigies are so called. So that, even if we regard Mopsus, Tiresias, Amphiaraus, Calchas, and Helenus as so many fictions of dramatic license —though even the dramas themselves would not have employed them as augurs, if the actual fact altogether rejected them—are we not taught even by instances at home to acknowledge the power of the Gods? Shall the recklessness of P. Claudius in the first Punic war have no effect upon us, when mocking the Gods merely in jest—as the chickens taken from the cage would eat nothing—he ordered them to be drowned, so that they might drink, as they refused to eat? That sneer, however, brought much sorrow to himself, through the defeat of the fleet, and heavy loss to the Roman people. Well? did not his colleague, Junius, in the same war, lose his fleet in a storm for having disobeyed the auspices? And so, Claudius was condemned by the people, and Junius sentenced himself to death.

'Cœlius mentions that, through neglect of religion, C. Flaminius fell at Trasimenus—with serious damage to the Republic. From the ruin of these men it may be inferred that the Republic was enlarged by the campaigns of those who obeyed religion; and, in fact, if we choose to compare ourselves with foreigners, we shall find ourselves, in other respects, equal or even inferior; but in religion, that is, in devotion to the Gods, far superior. Is that wand of Attus Nævius to be slighted, with which he defined the limits of a vineyard for tracking a sow? I would think so, had not King Hostilius, under his divination, waged his most important wars. But when, through negligence of the aristocracy, the strictness of augury was overlooked, the reality of auspices was disregarded and the form alone retained. Accordingly, the most important functions of the State, war included, on which the safety of the State depended, are managed without auspices. None of the long-established auspices are retained —the peremnia are disused—none from lance-heads—nor, when the selected men are summoned, since military testaments are no more. For it is since they have dispensed with the auspices that our generals are beginning to wage actual war. Among our ancestors, on the contrary, such was the influence of religion, that some commanders, veiling their heads, devoted themselves to the immortal Gods, with formal words, for the Republic. I could recall many of the Sybilline prophecies, many of the predictions of the haruspices, by which such facts would be established as could be doubted by none.

4. 'And, in fact, the event itself, in the consulship of P. Scipio and C. Figulus, proved the training of our own augurs and the Etruscan seers; for, when Tib. Gracchus, in his second consulship was nominating them; the first returning officer, as soon as he named them, fell dead suddenly on the spot. When Gracchus, notwithstanding that, concluded the election, and found that it had become a matter of conscience for the people, he reported it to the Senate. The Senate resolved that it be referred to the usual authorities. The haruspices, when brought in, pronounced that the returning officer had been irregular. Then Gracchus, as I used to hear from my father, provoked to anger, cried: "Is it so, indeed? Am I not in order, though I made the return as consul and under auspices? Can you—Etruscans and foreigners—know the law of Roman auspices and claim to be arbiters of our elections?" and accordingly ordered them to withdraw. Afterwards, however, he sent a letter from his province to his colleagues, stating that, on looking over the books, he recollected that the observatory—Scipio's Gardens—had been informally selected by him; because, when he afterwards entered the pomærium for the purpose of convening the Senate, he had forgotten, when crossing the pomærium again, on his way back, to take observations; and consequently that the consuls were informally elected. The augurs laid the case before the Senate. The Senate decided that the consuls should resign. They did resign. What better instances do we want? A most sensible man, and—for anything I know—the best of all men, would rather confess his error, though it might have been concealed, than that a matter of conscience should remain against the Republic; while the consuls chose to resign their supreme authority at once, rather than retain it a moment in defiance of religion. The authority of augurs is great. Well; is

not the art of the sacrifice-inspectors superhuman? And, whoever sees those countless instances of the same class, must he not be compelled to admit that there are Gods? Because those who are represented by interpreters, must themselves exist; but, there are interpreters of the Gods; and we must therefore acknowledge their existence. But then, perhaps all that is foretold does not come to pass. Because all patients do not recover, is there no medical science? Signs of coming events are shown by the Gods; and, if any mistakes are made respecting them, it is not the nature of the Gods, but the sagacity of men that is at fault. So that, among all men of every nation there is a coincidence of belief; for it is implanted, and, in a manner, engraved upon the mind, that there are Gods.

5. 'As to their attributes, opinions differ; their existence nobody denies. Cleanthes of our school, in fact, said that ideas of Gods are outlined in the human mind for these four reasons. First in order he placed that which I have just mentioned, founded upon the presentiment of future events; second, that which we infer from the extent of the benefits derived from the temperature of the atmosphere, the fertility of the soil, and the supply of many other conveniences; third, that which overawes the mind by lightning, rain-clouds, snow, hail, famine, pestilence, earthquakes, and frequent subterranean noises, showers of stones, and rain-drops like blood, landslips, or sudden opening of the earth, and unnatural monstrosities of men and beasts, the appearance of those stars which the Greeks call comets and our people *cincinnatæ*, which were recently, in the Octavian war, the forerunners of great calamities; by a double sun, which, as I heard from my father, appeared in the consulship of Tuditanus and Aquilius, in which year P. Africanus, one of our suns, was put out; by all which men were so terrified that they inferred the existence of a heavenly and superhuman power; fourth, and the strongest reason of all, the uniformity of motion, the revolution of the sphere, the regularity, diversity, beauty and arrangement of sun, moon and all stars, of which objects the mere sight would prove sufficiently that they are not the result of chance. As, if one were to come into a house, or gymnasium, or forum, he could not, on beholding the meaning, the method and system of everything, conclude that it all happened without a cause, but would understand that there is some one who

superintends it and is obeyed. Much more, in the case of such extensive motions and such mighty revolutions and the regularity of objects so immense in number and magnitude, in which measureless and infinite eternity has never exhibited an error, must he inevitably decide that physical revolutions on such a scale are guided by some intellect.

6. 'Chrysippus, indeed, though a man of most active mind, speaks in such a way that he seems to have learned from Nature itself instead of making his own discoveries. "Because, if there is anything," he says, "in the physical world that the intellect of man, that human reason, energy and power cannot do, the power that effects it is certainly higher than man. But the phænomena of astronomy and all those of which the arrangement is eternal, cannot be created by man, and therefore, that power by which they are perfected is more than human. And what can you call that power but God? And, in fact, if there are no Gods, what can there be in creation higher than man? For in him alone is reason, than which nothing can be more excellent. But the existence of any man who thinks nothing in the universe higher than himself is a case of stupid vanity. There is, then, something higher—there is certainly a God." Or, if you saw a large and decorated house, you could not be tempted to believe that it was built for rats and weasels; so then, would you not seem to be clearly insane, if you supposed that a world so highly embellished, such diversity and beauty of celestial objects, such might and magnitude of sea and land, was a home for yourself and not for the immortal Gods? Can we not understand even this, that what is higher is better; and, that the earth is lowest, as the densest atmosphere surrounds it?—and that, as for this reason the intellects of men are slower on account of the denser quality of the air—which we find to be the case of some countries and cities—the same effect is produced on the whole human race, because they are placed on the earth, that is, in the densest region of the universe; and, still, from the actual intelligence of man we must infer the existence of some intellect, and regard that as more active and superhuman. "Whence has man derived this?"—as Socrates, according to Xenophon, says. Besides, the moisture and heat that are diffused through the body, and even the earthy consistence of the flesh, and finally, this elastic breath—if anyone asks whence we have them, it is evident that we have got one

from the earth, another from water, another from fire; and the other from this air which we inhale by breathing.

7. 'But, that which surpasses all these—I mean reason; and, if you would have it under several names, mind, judgment, thought, wisdom—where have we found it? whence have we got it? Shall the world have all the rest, and not have this one which is of most value? And yet, certainly, nothing in all creation is better than the world. Not only is there nothing more excellent, nothing more beautiful, but nothing can be even imagined; and, if nothing is better than reason and wisdom, these must exist in that which we confess to be best. Well, then; whom should not such a coincident, uniform and unbroken relation of objects compel to accept what I say? Could the earth be at one time in bloom, and at another, bare of ornament? or, when so many objects are undergoing changes, could the approach and departure of the sun be known by the summer and winter solstices; or, the tides of the sea and the narrow straits be influenced by the rising and setting of the moon; or, the unequal orbits of the planets be maintained through one revolution of the sphere? All this could not result from mutual adaptation of all parts of the universe, if they were not controlled by one divine and pervading spirit. When these arguments are discussed more fully and expansively— as it is my intention to do—they escape the criticism of the Academics more easily. When, on the other hand, according to Zeno's custom, they are stated more shortly and concisely, they are more open to refutation. For, as a running stream is hardly, or never, while confined water is easily, tainted; so, by a torrent of words the censures of a disputant are washed away; while the closeness of condensed language cannot easily defend itself. These arguments, for instance, which I have expanded, Zeno used to condense in this way.

8. 'That which uses reason is better than that which does not; but nothing is better than the world: therefore it enjoys the use of reason. In like manner it can be proved that the world is wise—or happy—or immortal; for all these are better than what is destitute of them; and nothing is better than the world; by which it is proved that the world is God. He argues also in this form—No part of anything not sentient can be sentient; but parts of the world are sentient; the world then is not without sensation. He goes on still, and presses his argument more concisely—Nothing,

3—2

he says, that is destitute of mind and reason can produce from itself a living and rational being : but the world produces living and rational beings: therefore the world possesses life and intelligence. Still further, he winds up his argument, as he frequently does, with an analogy in this form— If flutes uttering musical sounds were to grow on an olive-tree, would you have any doubt that some knowledge of music existed in the tree? Well? If plane-trees produced stringed instruments vibrating musically, you would of course suppose that there was music in the trees. Why, then, should not the world be considered living and intelligent, as it produces from itself living and intelligent creatures?

9. 'But, since I have begun to treat the question differently from what I said at first—for I denied that this first proposition required discussion, as it must be evident to all that there are Gods—still, I wish to establish that very fact by proofs from physical science. For the case is this, that all things which receive nourishment and grow, contain internally the energy of heat without which they could neither be nourished nor grow. For everything that is hot and fiery is moved and agitated of itself; but what receives nourishment and grows, experiences a regular and uniform motion; and while this remains in us, so long do sensation and life remain; but, when it cools down and the heat escapes, we die and are extinguished. As, in fact, Cleanthes shows by these further arguments, what an amount of heat there is in every body; for he says that there is no food so heavy that it cannot be digested in a night and day, and that there is heat in even that refuse of it which nature rejects. Besides, the veins and arteries never cease to pulsate, as if by some fiery force; and it has been often observed that the heart of any animal torn out during life, pulsated so freely as to imitate the activity of fire. Everything, then, that has life, whether animal or issuing from the ground, lives by reason of the heat contained in it. And from this it must be inferred that the nature of heat has an intrinsic vital energy pervading the whole universe. This we shall see more plainly by explaining more minutely all this fiery principle which pervades everything. All parts of the universe, then—and I will allude to the most important—are maintained by the support of heat; and this can be perceived, especially, in the constitution of the earth; for we see fire struck out by the collision and friction of stones; and the soil, after recent digging,

exhaling its heat; and hot water drawn even from spring wells; and this occurring mostly in winter; because a large store of heat is enclosed in the cavities of the earth, and is more condensed in winter, and, for that reason, more closely confines the heat implanted in the earth.

10. 'It is a long discussion, and there are many arguments by which it may be shown that all things which the earth receives as seeds, and which self-propagated it holds attached by roots, derive their origin and growth from that modification of heat; and, that heat is present even in water, its transparency and fluidity prove; for it could neither be congealed by cold, nor be hardened by snow and frost, if it did not also become fluid by heat and melt away. Accordingly, under northerly winds and other forms of cold, moisture becomes solid, and is again softened and melted by the action of heat; and even the sea, when torn by the wind, grows so warm that it can be easily inferred that in such a mass of water heat is confined; for that warmth is to be regarded not as external and borrowed, but elicited by motion from the deepest regions of the sea; which is the case, also, in our own bodies when they grow warm by movement and exercise. But even the air, which is by nature especially cold, is by no means destitute of heat. It contains, in fact, a considerable mixture of heat, for its own origin is in the evaporation of water; because the vapour of this must be regarded as a sort of air, and results from the movement of the heat confined in water; and here we can see a resemblance in water that boils by the application of heat. Still further, the remaining fourth part of the world is torrid, and imparts to all other elements a healthy and vital heat: and hence comes the inference that, as all portions of the world are fed by heat, the world itself is kept alive, through such long duration, by an element alike in kind and degree; and, so much the more, as it must be understood that this hot and fiery principle is so diffused through all nature, that it comprises a power of generation and a cause of production, from which all living things, and those of which the roots are fixed in the earth, must necessarily derive their origin and growth.

11. 'There is, therefore, a native principle to embrace and guard the whole world, and this not without perception and reason; for it must be that every being that is not single and unmixed, but combined and connected with something else, has in itself some ruling principle; such as reason in

man, and in lower animals something resembling reason, from which arise various desires. In the case of trees and other products of the earth, the ruling principle is supposed to be seated in the roots. By a ruling principle I mean that which the Greeks call *hegemonicon*, than which nothing can or ought to be more excellent in the several categories; so that it is inevitable that what contains the ruling principle of all nature should be best of all, and of all things most worthy of power and dominion. We find also, that in portions of the globe—for there is nothing on all the globe that is not part of the whole—perception and reason exist. In that portion, therefore, in which dwells the ruling principle, these must of necessity be present in greater activity and quantity, for which reason the globe must of course be intelligent; and that principle which embraces and holds all things must excel in perfection of reason, and therefore must the globe be God and all its energy be centred in a divine principle; and that fiery action of the globe is also much purer, more transparent and diffusible, and for these reasons more suited to act upon our senses than this heat known to us, by which all that is familiar to us is perpetuated and strengthened. It is absurd, therefore, to say, when men and lower animals are pervaded by this heat, and thereby endowed with motion and sensation, that the globe is destitute of perception, though it is pervaded by an unmixed, pure, and free, and at the same time, most active and diffusible heat; especially, as that heat which belongs to the globe derives its motion, not from any other motion, nor from external impulse, but from itself and its own will: for, what can be stronger than a globe which drives out and gives motion to the heat by which it is pervaded?

12. 'Let us listen to Plato—a sort of God among philosophers—whose opinion is that motion is of two kinds—one intrinsic and the other external; and that spontaneous self-motion is more divine than what is set going by impulse from without. This latter motion he assigns to intellect alone, and believes that the origin of all motion is derived therefrom. For this cause, since all motion comes from the heat of the globe, and that heat moves not by external impulse but spontaneously, it must of course be intellect; and thus it is proved that the globe possesses life. From this it will also be perceived that intelligence exists in it,

because the globe is superior to any physical being. For, as there is no portion of our body that is not of less importance than ourselves; so, the whole globe must of course be more important than any part of it; and, this being so, the globe must be intelligent, because, if it were not so, man, although but a portion of the globe, would be, in right of his intellect, more important than the whole; and further, if we advance from primitive and rudimentary to final and perfect developments, we come inevitably to Gods; for, in the first instance, we find that the products of the earth are supported by nature, though nature does nothing more for them than to take care of them by nourishment and growth. To the lower animals, on the other hand, it gives sensation and motion with some degree of desire—a tendency to beneficial objects and repulsion from the destructive; but, to man this additional gift of reason, by which desires may be controlled, set free, and restrained alternately.

13. 'But the fourth, and the highest class comprises those who are by nature formed for goodness and wisdom, in whom is originally inborn true and consistent reason, which must be regarded as superhuman and the attribute of God, that is, the globe in which that perfect and transcendental reason must of necessity dwell. For it cannot be said that in any organized system there is not something final and perfect; as, for instance, in a vine, in a sheep, we find that, unless there is some counteracting force, nature attains its end in its own way; and, as painting and the constructive and other arts imply some realization of finished work, so, in every physical process and much more in these, there must be something thorough and perfect. Because many external obstacles may prevent other physical processes from being completed; but nothing can obstruct nature collectively, because it includes and contains all the subordinate agencies. Wherefore it must be that there is a fourth and highest class which no disturbance can reach. But it is that class in which the physical law of all things has its place; and, as this is so constituted that it governs all things, and nothing can obstruct it, the globe must of necessity possess intelligence and even wisdom. For, what can be a more stupid assertion than that the physical law which comprises all things, should not be called the most excellent; or, though it is most excellent, should not be, in the first place, endowed with life, and secondly, possessed of reason and judgment,

and finally, of wisdom? For, how otherwise could it be most excellent? Because, if it were like plants, or even lower animals, it could not be considered highest any more than lowest; nor, if it partakes of reason, and is still not originally wise, can the condition of the globe be regarded as not inferior to that of man; because man can acquire wisdom; but the globe, if it has been destitute of intelligence through all past eternity, can certainly never attain wisdom, and will therefore, be inferior to man. But, as that is absurd, the globe must be originally intelligent and be regarded as God. Because there is nothing else that exhibits no deficiency and is everywhere connected and perfect and finished in all proportions and details.

14. 'Chrysippus ingeniously remarks that, as the plating was invented for the sake of the shield, and the scabbard for the sword, so all things, except the globe, are produced for the sake of something else; as, for instance, the crops and fruits which the earth produces, for the use of animals; and other animals for the use of man, as the horse for bearing burdens, the ox for ploughing, the dog for hunting and watching. Man himself, however, is born to study and imitate the globe, not being at all perfect, but a small portion of that which is. But the globe, as it comprises everything, and there is nothing that is not contained in it, is thoroughly perfect. How, then, can the best of all things be wanting to it? Nothing is superior to intellect and reason. In these, therefore, the globe cannot be deficient. Truly, then, does Chrysippus argue, when, by the use of analogies, he shows that all qualities are better under conditions of maturity and perfection; as in the horse than in the colt, in the dog than in the whelp, in the man than in the boy; and further, that what is best in the whole globe, ought to be found in something perfect and complete. But nothing is more perfect than the globe itself, nothing better than virtue: virtue is, therefore, the special attribute of the globe. But human nature is not perfect, and yet virtue is exhibited in man. How much more easily, then, in the globe: virtue, therefore, dwells in it: and it is for that reason wise, and therefore a God.

15. 'Now, as this divinity of the globe is demonstrated, the same godhead must be assigned to the stars, which are produced from the most elastic and purest portion of the æther, are blended with no other element, are all fiery and

bright; so that these also may be most truly said to be animated, sentient, and intelligent: and that they are of a purely fiery nature Cleanthes believes to be proved by the evidence of the senses of touch and sight; because the light of the sun is brighter than any fire, shining as it does so far and widely from its immense disc, at the same time that its contact is such that it not only warms, but often burns: and neither of these effects could it produce unless it were fiery. "So that," he says, "as the sun is fiery and is fed by moisture from the ocean—because no fire can live without some fuel—it must of course resemble either that fire which we employ in cookery and other operations, or, that which is confined in the bodies of animals. But then, this ordinary fire which the purposes of life require, annihilates and devours all things, and, at the same time, alters and decomposes them. On the other hand, that animal heat, vital and conservative, preserves, nourishes, enlarges and supports all things and endows them with sensation." He says, accordingly, that there can be no doubt which of these the sun resembles; as it also causes all things to flourish and come to maturity in their several kinds. So that, as the sun's fire resembles those which are in the bodies of animals, the sun also must be animated; and, in fact, the other stars that rise in the celestial splendour called æther, or heaven. For, as the birth of some beings is on the earth, of some in the water, of others in the air, it seems to Aristotle absurd to suppose that no animal is produced in that element which is most suited to the production of animal life. But the stars have their place in æther; and, as that is the most rarefied and always in motion and action, it follows, of course, that any living being produced in it, must possess the quickest perception and the most rapid movement: so that, as the stars have their origin in the æther, it is reasonable that they should possess perception and intelligence; by which it is proved that they are to be counted as Gods.

16. 'For instance, we can observe that the intellects are sharper and more apprehensive, of those who inhabit those countries where the air is clear and thin, than of those who experience a thick and condensed atmosphere. It is even supposed that the food which we use makes some difference in the sharpness of the intellect. It is, therefore, probable that a high degree of intelligence should dwell in the stars which inhabit the æthereal region of the universe, and are

fed by exhalation from land and sea, rarefied by long distance. But, the arrangement and permanence of the stars is what most of all proclaims their perception and intelligence; for, there is nothing that can move systematically and harmoniously without judgment—in which nothing is undesigned, nothing changeable, nothing accidental : and the regularity of the stars and their permanence through all eternity imply neither unconscious action—for it is abundant in design—nor accident, which is allied to change and excludes permanence. It follows, then, that they move by their own will; their own perception and divine constitution. Nor is Aristotle to be denied praise for his theory, that all things that exhibit motion, move either by physical action, or force, or will; and, that the sun and moon and stars all move; but that, what is moved by physical action, either sinks by its own weight, or rises by its lightness, neither of which is the case with the stars ; because their motion is orbital and circular. Nor can it be said that it results from some superior force that the stars move independently of physical action ; for, what force could be superior? It remains, then, that their motion is voluntary : and, whoever sees all this would act not only stupidly but impiously, if he denied the existence of Gods. Nor does it make much difference whether he denies that fact, or denies them all supremacy and action ; for, one who does nothing seems to me to have no existence at all. The existence of Gods, therefore, is so manifest that whoever denies it, I scarcely consider of sound mind.

17. 'It now remains for us to consider what is their character ; and, in this inquiry, nothing is more difficult than to withdraw the mental view from the ordinary illusion of the eye. That difficulty has caused ignorant men and philosophers resembling them to be unable to form any conception of immortal Gods, except under the familiar form of man ; and the folly of this belief has been so exposed by Cotta as not to require discussion by me. But, when we are convinced by certain knowledge, first, that God is so constituted as to be animated ; and secondly, that nothing in all nature is more excellent, I see nothing that I can more properly adapt to this intuition and conception of ours, than to conclude, in the first place, that this globe, than which nothing more excellent can be produced, is animated and God. On this let Epicurus be as sarcastic as he pleases—well suited as he is to jesting, and by no means typical of his country—and

say that he cannot conceive the nature of a revolving and circular God; still, he shall never withdraw me from this belief, which he actually sanctions by his own : for, it is his belief that Gods exist, because there must inevitably be some being to which no other is superior. But nothing is more excellent than the globe; and there is no doubt that what is living and has perception and reason and intellect is superior to what is destitute of these. So it is proved that the globe is God. But all this will presently be more easily inferred from the effects of which the globe is the cause.

18. 'In the meantime, Velleius, do not, I beg, profess that your sect is totally destitute of learning. You say that a cone, or a cylinder, or a pyramid seems to you more symmetrical than a sphære. Your visual taste is peculiar : but, let us suppose these forms more beautiful merely to the eye, though even that is not my estimate; for what can surpass in beauty that form which comprises in itself all others, and can have no unevenness, no flaw, nothing angular or tortuous, no projection, no depression ? And, as these are the two most perfect figures—the globe—for so we choose to translate *sphaira*—among solids, and among plane figures, the circle or orb, which in Greek is called *kuklos;* of these two figures alone it is true that all their segments exactly resemble each other, and that the outline is all equidistant from the centre; than which nothing can be more symmetrical. But, if you do not see this, as you have never studied those scientific diagrams, have you not been able to understand so much of physical science—that this uniformity of motion and permanence of regularity could not be maintained in any other form ? So that nothing can imply greater ignorance than what is habitually asserted by you—for, you say that it is not certain that this world is round, because it is possible that it may have some other form ; and that countless other worlds may be of various forms—which Epicurus would certainly not say, if he had learned how much twice two make. But, while he decides what is best for the palate, he has not looked up—as Ennius says—at "the palate of the sky."

19. 'For, as there are two classes of stars, of which one, travelling from east to west in an unvarying course, never reverse the direction of their motion, while the other accomplishes two successive revolutions in the same course and orbit; from both these facts the revolution of the globe—

which is consistent only with a circular form—and the circular orbits of the stars are ascertained: and, in the first place, the sun, which holds the highest rank among stars, moves in such a manner that it illumines alternately one side of the earth, while it leaves the other in darkness; because the earth's own shadow intercepting the sun-light, causes night; and the uniformity of the intervals of darkness and of daylight is the same. Of the sun, also, the approaching and receding alternations modify heat and cold. His annual revolution occupies 365 days, with an additional fourth of a day. Inclining his orbit to north and south alternately, he produces summer and winter, with the two seasons, of which one follows the decline of summer, the other that of winter: so that, from these four changes of season, the first origin of all productions of sea and land proceeds. The moon, next, completes every month the same revolution which the sun performs in a year. Its nearest approach to the sun produces the faintest illumination, and its greatest distance the fullest. Nor are its phases alone changed in filling and waning by returning to the first quarter; but its position also, which is alternately northern and southern. In the motion of the moon there is, also, some analogy to a summer and winter solstice, and many influences emanate and proceed from it, by which animals are nourished and products of the earth grow and become reproductive and attain maturity.

20. 'Most wonderful, however, are the motions of the five stars, erroneously called wanderers; for there is really no wandering in that which, through all eternity, maintains its forward and retrograde motions and other revolutions constant and established. And this is more wonderful in those stars of which we are speaking, for this reason, that alternately they appear and disappear, advance and retreat, precede and follow, move faster and more slowly, show no motion at all, and stand still for an interval. From all these various movements, mathematicians have given the name of the great year to the period in which the return of the sun and moon and five planets to their original relative position is effected by the completion of all their orbits. How long this period is, forms an important question; but it must of course be definite and fixed. The star, for instance, known as Saturn, and called *Phainon* by the Greeks, and the most distant from the earth, completes its orbit in about thirty years, and in that revolution exhibits many wonderful movements, alter-

nately progressing and delaying, disappearing in the evening and shining out again in the morning, and shows no variation in the same periodic movements through all the ages of eternity. Inside this and nearer to the earth is the star of Jupiter, called *Phaeton*, and this traverses the same orbit through the twelve signs in twelve years, and exhibits in its revolution the same phases as Saturn. The orbit next to and inside this is that of *Pyroeis*, which is called Mars; and this performs the same revolution as the superior planets in twenty-four months, wanting, I believe, six days. Inside this is Mercury, called by the Greeks, *Stilbon*, which, in about a year, travels its path through the zodiac, and is never more distant from the sun than the space of one sign, whether preceding or following. The lowest of the five planets and the nearest to the earth, is the star of Venus, called in Greek, *Phosphoros*, and in Latin, Lucifer, when it precedes the sun, and Hesperus when it follows. This completes its revolution in one year, traversing the length and breadth of the zodiac, as the superior planets also do, and never goes further from the sun, preceding or following, than the space of two signs.

21. 'This regularity of the planets, and uniformity of time in their several revolutions through all eternity, unless by intellect, reason and design, I cannot conceive; and, when we find these in the stars, we cannot refuse to classify them as Gods. Nor, indeed, do those stars that are called "fixed," fail to indicate the same intelligence and wisdom; for their daily movement is uniform and constant, and they have no æthereal or orbital motion, as many suppose, through ignorance of physical science: for the æther is not so constituted as to be able, by intrinsic force, to hold and rotate the stars: thin and transparent and penetrated by an even temperature, it seems not well suited to take hold of stars. Accordingly, the fixed stars have a sphere of their own, apart from and independent of relation to the æther. Their eternal and incessant movements, however, in their wonderful and inconceivable permanence, prove that they possess force and divine intelligence; so that, whoever cannot perceive that these also have the power of Gods, seems not likely to perceive anything whatever. There is, therefore, in the heavens neither accident nor hazard, nor wandering, nor insignificance: on the contrary, all is regularity, truth, system, uniformity, and such as are destitute of these, deceptive, delusive and misleading, have their place below the moon, which is the

lowest of all, about and on the earth. So that, whoever supposes that this wonderful and inconceivable regularity and permanence, on which the preservation and safety of all entirely depends, are independent of intelligence, must be regarded as deficient in intellect. I will not, therefore, I think, go astray, if I begin with our Master in searching out the truth of this question.

22. 'Zeno, then, defines Nature by calling it a creative fire and proceeding directly to production; for he believes that it is the special function of art to create and produce; and that, whatever the hand effects in human art, Nature accomplishes much more artistically, *i.e.*, as I said, the creative fire, the teacher of all other arts. On this principle, in fact, all Nature is artistic; because it may be said to have a road and a path to follow. But, the nature of the globe itself, which holds in its embrace and contains everything, is described by Zeno as not merely mechanic, but artistic, suggesting and foreseeing all advantages and opportunities: and as all other natures are produced from their several germs, and grow, and are contained in them; so, the nature of the globe has all its motions subject to its will; as, also, those tendencies and desires which the Greeks call *hormœ*, and suits its actions to these, as we do who are moved by thought and sensation: so that, as the intellect of the globe is of this sort, and for that reason may be called *prudence* or *providence*—for, it is called, in Greek, *pronoia*—it provides especially for and employs itself principally in this: that, in the first place, the globe may be best adapted to a condition of permanence; secondly, that it may want nothing; and most of all, that it may exhibit exquisite beauty and all embellishment.

23. 'The globe in all its relations has been described: the stars also have been described; so that, now, there appears almost a multitude of Gods who are neither idle, nor perform what they do with hard and distressing work; because they are not embodied in veins and nerves and bones, nor do they consume such food and drink as to produce fluids too fine or too coarse; nor inhabit such bodies that they dread falls or blows, or apprehend sickness from the exhaustion of their strength; for it was through fear of these accidents that Epicurus represented his Gods shadowy and inactive. The former, on the contrary, enjoying the greatest beauty of form and placed in the purest region of the heavens, so move and regulate their revolutions that they seem, by a mutual under-

standing, to preserve and maintain the whole. But, many other classes of Gods have been set up and named by the wisest of the Greeks and our ancestors, and deservedly, for important services; because they supposed that whatever confers great benefit on mankind, could not happen without divine benevolence; and therefore identified with the name of the God whatever originated with him; as, when we speak of corn as Ceres, and wine as Liber; whence that saying of Terence—" Without Ceres and Liber, Venus starves." Then, the object in which there is any more active quality, is so named that the abstract quality is called a God: Fides and Mens, for instance, which we see recently canonized in the Capitol by M. Æmilius Scaurus. Fides had been previously deified by Atilius Calatinus. You see the temple of Virtus, and that of Honor, which was consecrated many years before, during the Ligurian war, by Q. Maximus, restored by M. Marcellus. Why mention the temples of Ops, of Salus, Concordia, Libertas, and Victoria? And because of all these the qualities are such that, except by a God, they could not be controlled, they have themselves obtained the rank of Gods. In this class, the names of Cupido and Voluptas and Venus Libitina have been consecrated—vicious and unnatural as they are, though Velleius thinks differently. Vices, however, often exert a powerful influence upon Nature. For the value of their services, therefore, those men who conferred the several benefits have been set up as Gods: and by the names just now mentioned, the qualities distinguishing the several Gods are indicated.

24. 'The experience of mankind, however, and popular custom, adopted the principle of promoting to heaven men distinguished for their services, by celebrity and choice. From this custom resulted Hercules and Castor and Pollux and Æsculapius. Hence also Liber—I mean Liber the son of Semele, not him whom our ancestors solemnly and reverently deified with Ceres and Libera—and what that means can be learned from the mysteries. But, as we call our own children *liberi*, for that reason the children of Ceres have been named Liber and Libera; which is still retained in the case of Libera, though not with respect to Liber. Hence also Romulus, whom they identify with Quirinus: for as their souls survived and enjoyed immortality, they are properly regarded as Gods, being most excellent and immortal.

'From another, and, in fact, a physical cause, a large number of Gods has proceeded, who, clothed in human form, supplied the poets with legends and filled human life with all sorts of superstition. This topic, handled by Zeno, has been illustrated at full length by Cleanthes and Chrysippus. An old superstition, for instance, pervaded Greece, to this effect—that Cœlus was mutilated by his son Saturn, and Saturn himself imprisoned by his son Jupiter. A physical principle has been not ungracefully disguised in an irreverent fable; for they supposed that the highest æthereal—that is, the fiery—element, which produced all things of itself, should be independent of that portion of the body which requires for procreation the help of another sex.

25. 'Saturn, again, they regarded as the controller of the course and revolutions of periods of time; and the God bears that name in Greek, being called *Kronos*, which is the same as *Chronos*—that is, a length of time; but, he bears the name of Saturn, because he fills himself—*saturatur*—with years; as he is represented in the habit of devouring his children; for duration eats up intervals of time and gorges itself insatiably with past years; and, on the other hand, chained by Jupiter, to restrict him from unlimited movement and to confine him within the bonds of the stars. But Jupiter himself—that is, *Juvans pater*—whom, by an irregular declension, we call Jove—from *juvando*—is styled by the poets " father of Gods and men," and by our ancestors, " best and greatest." And, in fact, *best*—that is, most beneficent—in precedence of *greatest;* because it is a higher and more gracious quality to be a benefactor to all, than to possess great power. Him, accordingly, Ennius, as I said above, names, when he says, " Behold this empyrean height, whom all address as Jove," more plainly than he elsewhere says—" To whom, with all the power I have, I will pray—this source of light, whatever it is." To him our augurs also allude, when they speak of " Jove flashing," for they mean " the sky flashing and thundering." Euripides, too, with his usual felicity, speaks briefly thus—" See you the expansive boundless sky, that clasps the earth in soft embrace? This regard as the supreme God. To this give the name of Jove."

26. 'The air, as the Stoics argue, separating sea and sky, is deified under the name of Juno, who is the sister and consort of Jove; because it resembles and has the closest connection with æther. They have, however, called it female, and

assigned it to Juno; because there is nothing more yielding. But, I believe that Juno takes her name from *juvando*. Water and earth were the remaining elements, to form—according to mythology—three separate kingdoms. To Neptune, accordingly, the second brother, as they believe, of Jupiter, all the dominion of the sea was given, with a lengthened name. As Portunus from *portu;* so comes Neptunus from *nando*, by a slight change of the first letters; but, all the power and productive energy of the earth was devoted to father Dis, who is called Dives—as he is by the Greeks, *Plouton;* because all things return to and issue from the earth. To him they say that Proserpina was married, whose name is the same that is called in Greek *Persephone;* and they mean that she is the seed of corn, and when buried, is sought by her mother; and her mother Ceres—that is, *Geres*—takes her name from *gerendis*—bearing the crops: the first letter being accidentally changed, as in Greek; for there she is called *Demeter*, equivalent to *Gemeter*. Mars is he who—*magna vertit*—causes great revolutions, and Minerva—*minuit* v. *minatur*—diminishes or menaces.

27. 'And as, in all things, the beginning and the end have the greatest influence, they intended Janus to have the first place in sacrificing; because his name comes from *eundo*—going on; whence all passages are called *Jani;* and the entrance-doors of unconsecrated buildings are named *Januæ*. The name of Vesta is of Greek origin; for she is called by them *Hestia;* and her influence relates to altars and hearths. Accordingly, in that Goddess who is the guardian of the household, all worship and sacrifice have their end. Not far removed from this influence are the Penates, whose name is derived either from *penu*—for, all human food is *penus*—or, from residing within—*penitus;* whence the name *Penetrales* given by the poets. The name of Apollo, regarded as the Sun, is Greek: and Diana and Luna are considered the same; while the sun—*sol*—is so called, either because, of all the stars, he is alone—*solus*—in magnitude; or because, when he rises, he outshines the rest, and is alone visible: and the moon—*Luna*—is so named from *lucendo*—shining; for she is the same as *Lucina;* and therefore, as among the Greeks, they invoke, in child-birth, Diana, who is also *Lucifera*, so, among our people, they call upon Juno Lucina; and the same Diana is called *omnivaga*—all pervading; not from hunting—*venando;* but, because

she is included in the seven wandering stars—*vagantibus*—and named Diana; because, at night, she makes a sort of day. She is invited to births, because they come to maturity sometimes in seven, or, at most, in nine revolutions of the moon; and these, because they accomplish a measured—*mensa*—course, are called months—*menses*—and Timæus, with his usual wit, when he mentioned in his history, that, in the same night when Alexander was born, the temple of the Ephesian Diana was burnt, added that it was nothing wonderful; because Diana, as she wanted to assist Olympias, was away from home. But the Goddess who comes—*venit*—to all creatures, our people have named Venus; and from her name comes *venustas*—loveliness—rather than the name from it.

28. 'You perceive then, how, from physical facts, successfully and profitably discovered, ideas have been transferred to unreal and imaginary Gods? And this has produced erroneous theories and complicated mistakes, and superstitions almost suited to old women; for instance, the forms of Gods and their ages and costumes and decorations are familiar to us; their parentage, also, and marriages and family connections, are all assimilated to the weakness of human nature; because they are suggested to minds equally confused; because we have heard of the desires and vexations, and anger of Gods; nor, as legends record, have they been exempt from war and battle; not only when, as in Homer, Gods on different sides championed opposing armies; but they have even waged wars of their own, as with Titans and Giants. All this is told and most stupidly believed, and abounds in absurdity and the utmost folly. And still, when these fables are discredited and rejected, a Deity can be conceived, pervading the constitution of everything—Ceres of the earth, Neptune of the sea, and others of other elements: and these, such as they are, and under the names which custom has given them, we are bound to respect and worship as Gods. But the best and, at the same time, the most sincere and holy and devotional worship of the Gods is this—that we should revere them always with a purity and entireness and disinterestedness of thought and word; because not philosophers only, but our ancestors, have distinguished religion from superstition. Those persons, for instance, who used to pray and make offerings all day long, that their children might enjoy long life, were called superstitious; though the

name had, eventually, a wider application. Those, on the other hand, who carefully handled and—so to say—selected everything relating to the worship of the Gods, were called religious—from *religendo*—as diligent comes from *diligendo*; intelligent from *intelligendo*; for all these words involve the same idea of selection—*legendi*—that we find in "religious." So it happens that, of the two words superstitious and religious, one implies a defect and the other a virtue. And now, I believe I have satisfactorily shown that there are Gods, and what their attributes are.

29. 'What comes next is that I should prove that the world is governed by divine providence. The topic is certainly extensive, and debated by your sect, Cotta, and of course the controversy is altogether with you; for to your sect, Velleius, it is not so well known how the several details are treated, because you read only your own treatises, and are satisfied with them: others you condemn unheard; as you said yesterday, that a fortune-telling crone Pronœa—that is, Providence—was introduced by the Stoics. That you said under the mistaken impression that providence was invented by them as a sort of individual Goddess, to govern and rule the whole world; but the phrase is incomplete; as if one were to say that the Athenian Republic is ruled by a Council, "of the Areopagus" would be understood; so, when we say that the world is ruled by providence, you are to understand "of the Gods." Fully and completely, however, you are to understand the phrase in this sense—that the world is governed by the providence of the Gods. Do not, therefore, waste that salt, in which your country is deficient, in ridiculing us; and, in fact, if you take my advice, you would not even make the attempt—it does not suit you—it is not your gift—you can't do it. Nor, indeed, is this remark applied to you in particular—a man polished by home discipline and the refinement of the present generation—but, to the rest of your sect, and to him in particular who originated that doctrine—a person without science, without literature, offensive to all—destitute of taste, prestige, and wit.

30. 'I say, then, that it is by divine providence that the world and all its details have been originally arranged and are governed throughout all time, and the proof of that, one sect generally divide into three propositions; of which the first is the inference from the argument which shows that there are Gods; and, when this is granted, it must be

admitted that the world is governed by their wisdom. The second is, that which proves that all things are under the control of a sentient nature, and are most successfully managed by it: and when that is established, it follows that it is itself produced by life-giving elements. The third topic is the inference from appreciation of the phænomena of heaven and earth.

'In the first place, then, either it must be denied that there are Gods—and Democritus and Epicurus, by suggesting, respectively, optical delusions and phantoms, do, to some extent, deny it—or, it must be confessed by those who admit the existence of Gods, that they must do something, and that on a grand scale. There can be nothing grander than the government of the world: it is governed, therefore, by the wisdom of the Gods; and, if it is otherwise, there must be something higher and invested with greater power than the Gods, of what sort soever it may be, whether inanimate nature, or, destiny set in motion by a great force, and accomplishing these most beautiful works which we see. The power of the Gods, in that case, cannot be supreme or paramount, if it is controlled either by that destiny, or, the physical law by which heaven, sea and earth are ruled. But there is nothing higher than God, and the world must, therefore, be ruled by him. He is, therefore, controlled by and obeys no physical law, and therefore rules all Nature. For, if we admit that the Gods are intelligent, we admit, also, that they exercise a providence over the most important interests. Do they, then, not know what interests are most important, and how they should be administered and guarded, or, have they no power to maintain and govern affairs of such importance? But, ignorance is inconsistent with the character of Gods, while inability to discharge a duty can never be attributed to their Majesty.

31. 'And it must be, since Gods exist—if only they do, as they certainly do—that they are living, and not only living, but intelligent, and united among themselves by a sort of political unity and fellowship, ruling the world as a whole, like a common republic and city. It follows that the same intelligence belongs to them as to the human race; the same mutual sincerity, and the same law, which is the preference of right and aversion from wrong. From this it is inferred that wisdom and intellect came from God to man; and that, consequently, under the custom of our ancestors,

intellect, fidelity, valour, concord, were canonized and nationally established. And how can it be consistent to deny that these are attributes of Gods, when we worship their venerable and sacred portraits? So that, if among mankind there exist intellect, fidelity, valour and concord, whence but from higher beings could these descend to the earth? And, as prudence, reason and wisdom exist in us, the Gods must possess them in a higher degree; and not merely possess them, but employ them also for the best and greatest purposes. But there is nothing greater or better than the globe. It must be, then, that it is governed by the wisdom and providence of the Gods. Finally, as I have proved clearly that these are Gods whose visible power and light-giving presence we see—the Sun, I mean, and Moon and planets and fixed Stars, and the sky and the globe itself, and the actions of the objects contained in it, with great profit and convenience to mankind—it is established that they are all ruled by divine intelligence and wisdom—of the first proposition enough has been said.

32. 'The next topic is that I show you that everything is under the control of nature, and is most successfully managed by it. But, what nature itself is must be first briefly explained; so that what I want to prove may be more easily understood. Some believe that nature is an unreasoning force, producing compulsory movements in masses of matter. Others, again, that it is an intelligent force, proceeding in a systematic course, and proclaiming what it does and why, and with what result; whose skill no science, no dexterity, no mechanic can ever attain by imitation, and that the energy of seed is such that, however small it may be, yet, if it finds physical conditions to receive and hold it, and obtains matter from which it can receive nourishment and growth, it so forms and produces everything according to its kind, that some are fed by their own stems, and others can move and feel, and desire, and produce others in their own likeness. There are, still, others who call everything by the name of Nature; Epicurus, for instance, who classifies them in this way—that the nature of all things includes matter and space and their accessories. We, however, when we assert that the globe consists of and is governed by Nature, speak of it not as we would of a clod or a piece of stone, or anything of that sort; but, as we speak of a tree, or an animal, in which

is exhibited not chance, but organization and some semblance of design.

33. 'So that, if those plants which are held in the earth by their stems, live and flourish by the design of Nature, certainly, the earth itself is connected with the same force by the same design; because, when impregnated by seed, it gives birth to and yields all products from itself, and clasping their stems, feeds and enlarges them, and is, itself, in turn, fed by elements from above and without. By its exhalations, also, the air and æther and all the upper regions are fed: and so, if the earth is occupied by and derives strength from Nature, the same system prevails in the rest of the globe. For, plants are fixed in the earth, and, while they live, are supported by breathing air, and the air itself assists us in seeing and hearing and being heard; because none of these functions can dispense with it. Still further, it moves with us; for, wherever we go, wherever we move, it seems as if to give way and yield: and whatever elements gravitate to the central region of the globe—which is the lowest—and all that tends upward from the centre, and whatever revolves in orbital motion round the centre, all these constitute a cosmic system continuous and undivided.

'And, as there are four elementary bodies, it is by their mutual action that the system is perpetuated; because, from earth comes water, from water air, from air æther; and then, back again, from æther comes air, then water, and from water the earth below. So, from those elements of which all things consist, moving upward and downward, to and fro, the unity of the parts of the globe is effected. These elements must be either eternal, under this arrangement that we see, or, at least, enduring for some long and almost incalculable time. Whichever of these is the fact, it follows that the globe is governed by physical law. For, what navigation of ships or drilling of an army, or—to return to the analogy of what Nature does—what propagation of vine or tree, or, further, what organization of an animal, or formation of limbs, implies so much design of nature as the globe itself? Either there is nothing, therefore, that is directed by an intelligent nature, or, it must be admitted that the globe is so directed: for how can it be that what includes all other creatures and their seeds, is itself otherwise than governed by physical law? As, if one were to say that the teeth and the procreative power existed by nature, and that man himself, for whose benefit they exist, is not organized by nature, he would fail to understand that those beings which produce others from themselves, have a higher organization than what is produced from them.

34. 'But, of all things that are ordered by nature, the globe is the sower and planter and parent, and—so to speak—the trainer and feeder; and nurses and holds them all, as so many members and portions of itself; so that, if parts of the globe are ordered by nature, the globe itself must be so ordered, as its government involves nothing that can be censured; for of all the materials at hand, the best possible has been made. Let any man show that it could have been better. But this no one will ever show; and whoever desires to improve anything, will either make it worse, or will require what is impossible. If, then, all details of the system are so arranged that they could be neither more serviceable in use, nor more beautiful to the eye, let us consider whether they are the result of chance, or, in such a position that they could in no way co-exist, but under the control of an intelligent and divine providence. If, then, the works of Nature are superior to those of Art, and if Art can do nothing without intelligence, not even Nature can be supposed to be independent of intelligence. How, then, is it consistent, when you look upon a statue or a picture, to know that art has been employed; and, when you watch, far away, the course of a ship, to have no doubt that it is guided by scientific skill: or, when you look at a sundial or water-clock, to perceive that the hours are marked by science and not by chance; and yet, to suppose that the globe, which comprises all those arts, and their professors and all else, is destitute of wisdom and reason? If one were to take to Scythia or to Britain that orrery which our friend Poseidonius recently constructed, of which every revolution exhibits, in the sun, moon, and five planets, the same movement that takes place in the heavens every day and night; who, even among those savages, would doubt that the orrery was constructed by intelligent design?

35. 'These men, however, are in doubt respecting the globe, from which all things have their origin and being; whether it has been formed by chance, or, by some fatality, or, by divine reason and intellect, and suppose that Archimedes succeeded better in imitating the revolutions of the planetary system, than Nature in producing them; especially

when, in many particulars, the original work is more ingenious than the imitation; and yet, that shepherd in Accius, who had never before seen a ship, when he descried from the mountain the strange and superhuman conveyance of the Argonauts, in his first amazement and alarm, speaks to this effect: "So large a mass glides on, hissing from the deep with loud noise and vigour. It drives the waves before it, and makes whirlpools by its force. Onward it rushes, scattering the waves, and roars. Now, one would fancy that a bursting rain-cloud rolls on; now that a rock, forced on by wind and tempest, was cast on high; or, that the whirlwind arose, struck by the clash of waves. But, perhaps, the sea is making ruin of the land; or Triton with his trident is opening up his cave, and loosens from its roots the rock, torn from the depths, to the open air."

'He is at first in doubt what that object is, which he sees but knows not: and yet, when he sees the men and hears the sailor's song: "So do the rushing and sportive dolphins roar with their snouts"—and many other comparisons—"it brings to the ear a song and a noise like the music of Sylvanus."

'So that, as he, on the first view, thinks he beholds some lifeless and mindless object; but, afterwards, from plainer indications, begins to suspect the character of the subject of his doubts; so ought philosophers, if the first sight of the globe astonishes them, to understand afterwards—on seeing its regular and even movements, and everything controlled by established succession and unvarying punctuality—that there is, in this heavenly mansion, not only an inhabitant, but a master and ruler; and, in some sense, an architect of so vast a work and so great a responsibility.

36. 'As it is, however, they seem to me not even to suspect how wonderful are the phænomena of the heavens and the earth. In the first place, the earth, set in the central region of the system, is surrounded everywhere by this vital element which we breathe and call *air*. The name is Greek, but now adopted by our people; and is commonly used as Latin. This, in turn, the boundless *æther* encloses, which consists of the highest fire. Let us borrow this phrase also; and let *æther*, as well as *air*, be Latin: though Pacurius translates it—"This, that I mention, our people call *sky*, and the Greeks *æther*"—as if it were not Greek that he is speaking. But he is talking Latin; that

is, if we can hear him and not fancy that he is talking Greek. He gives us the same information in another passage—"a Greek: this his accent proves."

'However, let us come back to more important matter. From the æther, then, countless blazing stars shine out, of which the chief is the Sun, shedding most brilliant light on everything; many times larger than the whole earth: after him, other stars of immeasurable size: and, these fires, so large and so many, not only do no injury to the earth and earthly objects, but are beneficial, under such conditions that if they were displaced, the earth would inevitably be burnt, when so much heat was released from control and restraint.

37. 'Here, should I not be astonished to find any one who could satisfy himself that some solid and separate objects are moved by their intrinsic force and weight, and that a globe, perfect in its accessories and beauty, is formed by the accidental combination of those bodies? I cannot understand why whoever thinks this possible, should not also believe that, if countless types of the one and twenty letters, made of gold or other material, were thrown in a heap anywhere, the Annals of Ennius might be legibly composed, though I don't know that chance could effect so much even with a single line. But, on what principle do those persons assert that from atoms possessing neither colour nor any other quality—which the Greeks call *poiotes*—nor perception, but combining by chance and at random, a world has been formed: or, rather that, in countless numbers and in every second of time, some come into being and others perish? But, if a combination of atoms can make a world, why can it not build a colonnade, a temple, a house, or a city? For all these are less complicated and more easy. At least, they talk such reckless nonsense about the globe, that they seem to me to have never raised their eyes to this wonderful garniture of the heavens, which is my next topic. That is, therefore, a fine illustration which Aristotle supplies—"If there were," he says, "beings who had always lived underground in good and handsome houses that were furnished with statues and paintings, and all those things which they have who are considered wealthy; and yet, had never come out on the surface; but had heard by tradition and hearsay of some divine influence and power of the Gods; and were, then, on some occasion, enabled by the opening of the jaws of the earth to issue from that covered abode, and come out

upon the region that we inhabit—when they suddenly got sight of land and sea and sky, and observed the size of the clouds and the force of the wind, and beheld the sun, and became acquainted with his size and beauty and utility in making day by shedding his light over the whole sky; and saw, when night cast its shadow upon the earth, the heaven all spangled and beautified with stars, and the changing phases of the moon, when filling and waning, and the rising and setting of all these bodies, and their regular and unvarying motions through all time—seeing all this, they would, of course, conclude that there are Gods, and that such works as these are divine."

38. 'This is what he says. But, let us imagine such darkness as is said to have, on one occasion, from an eruption of the fire of Ætna, enveloped all the neighbouring district, so that, for two days, no man could recognise another; and, on the third, when the sun shone out, they felt as if restored to life. But, if the same change occurred, after an eternity of darkness, and we suddenly saw light, what would the view of the sky seem to us? But, through daily habit and the familiarity of sight, our minds become used to it, and feel neither astonishment nor curiosity respecting the causes of what we constantly see; as if novelty rather than the scale of the phænomena ought to urge us to investigate the causes. Who, for instance, would credit him with human intelligence, who, after seeing such regular movements of heavenly bodies, such a permanent arrangement of stars and so much mutual combination and adaptation, could deny that there is some design in them, and say that they are the result of chance; though we can by no power of thought realize the wisdom with which they are managed? When we see something moving mechanically—an orrery, for instance, or a clock, or many other machines—we never doubt that they are works of design; but, when we behold the revolution of the heavens, moving with miraculous speed and revolving with the utmost punctuality, maintaining their annual periods, for the safety and preservation of all things; can we doubt that all this is done not only by design, but a design remarkable and superhuman? For we can, now, laying aside critical controversy, observe to some extent with our eyes, the beauty of all that we describe as established by divine providence.

39. 'In the first place, let us survey the whole earth, set in

the centre of the universe, solid and circular and rounded everywhere by its own gravitation, clothed with flowers, grass, trees and crops, of all which the inconceivable number is diversified by endless variety. Add to these the cool and perennial fountains, the transparent waters of rivers, the verdure that clothes the banks, the hollow domes of caverns, the ruggedness of rocks, the height of overhanging mountains, the boundless extent of plains: add, also, the buried veins of gold and silver, and the inexhaustible supplies of marble. But, of animals, tame and wild, how many and various species! What flying and singing of birds! What feeding of cattle! What life in the forests! What can I say of the human race? For these, being appointed—so to say—cultivators of the earth, suffer it neither to be desolated by the ferocity of wild beasts, nor made barren by the roughness of the jungle; and by their industry the fields, islands, and sea-coasts are dotted and embellished with houses and cities; and if we could see all this with our mental vision, as we see it with our eyes, no man, contemplating the whole earth, could have a doubt of the divine intelligence.

'But, how perfect the beauty of the sea, and the effect of it taken as a whole! What a number and diversity of islands, and what scenery of coast and shore! How many and different species of animals, some living in the depths, some on the surface and swimming, some holding on to the rocks by their native shells! While the sea itself, embracing the land, so encloses it with its shores that, of the combination of the two elements one seems to be formed. Then, the atmosphere of the seaside changes by day and night; and sometimes, rarefied and expanded, floats upward, and again, when condensed, is massed into clouds, and attracting moisture, feeds the earth with showers, and, moving to and fro, produces wind. It also produces annual vicissitudes of cold and heat, and at the same time supports the flight of birds, and, inhaled by breathing, nourishes and maintains animal life.

40. 'What remains is the farthest and highest above our dwelling-place, surrounding all and enclosing the concavity of the sky, which is called æther; the utmost limit and boundary of the universe, in which, most wonderfully, fiery forms mark out their destined course. Of these, the sun, by which the earth is many times exceeded in size, revolves round it; and by its rising and setting produces day and

4—2

night; and receding and approaching alternately, makes two revolutions in opposite directions, from the tropics, every year. By these periodic motions, it now darkens the earth with a sort of sadness, and again gladdens it in compensation, so that it seems to borrow a brightness from the sky. Then, the moon, which is, as astronomers tell us, larger than half the earth, moves in the same course with the sun, but sometimes in conjunction with and sometimes receding from him, reflects upon the earth the light which she receives from him, and shows various phases of illumination; and, sometimes passing between us and the sun, eclipses and darkens his light; and sometimes, falling within the shadow of the earth, when it is between her and the sun, suddenly fades out, through the interposition and intervention of the earth. In the same course, those stars that we call planets, revolve round the earth, and rise and set in the same way; as their motion is alternately accelerated and retarded and sometimes ceases altogether. Than this sight nothing can be more wonderful or beautiful. Next comes the large multitude of fixed stars, of which the map is so accurately drawn, that they have acquired names from their resemblance to familiar forms.'

41. At this point, looking at me, he said:

'I will quote those lines of Aratus, which were translated by you in your young days, and please me so much, as they are in Latin, that I still remember many of them. Therefore, as we constantly see plainly, without any change or variation:

'"The other heavenly bodies pursue their course in rapid motion,
And, with the sky, revolve by day and night."

Of observing these no man's mind can tire, who wishes to see the punctuality of Nature.

'"And the final point of each extremity is called the pole."

Round this the two bears revolve and never set—

'"Of these, one is named by the Greeks, Cynosura, and the other, Helicé"—

whose most brilliant constellations we see every night—

'"Which our people usually call the seven Triones."

And with the same number of stars, similarly defined, the little Cynosura illumines the same pole—

> "On this the Phœnicians rely as their nightly guide at sea,
> Though the former, rising first, shines more brightly, studded with stars,
> And is seen at once from early nightfall:
> This is small, but mariners know its use,
> For it revolves in a smaller and more central orbit."

42. 'And, in order that the appearance of these stars may be more wonderful—

> "Between them, like a river with swift stream,
> The grim Dragon creeps, coiling himself above and below;
> And bends his body into winding folds."

Though his appearance is, on the whole, remarkable, the form of his head and the flash of his eyes are especially worthy of notice—

> "To adorn his head not one star merely shines;
> But his temples are marked with twofold fire,
> And from his fierce eyes burn two glowing lights;
> And his chin is bright with one flaming star.
> His head is bowed, and bent on his rounded neck,
> His gaze seems fixed on the tail of the greater Bear."

The rest of the Dragon's body we see every night—

> "Here suddenly the head hides itself a while
> Where the seen and unseen parts unite in one."

And the head itself—

> "Is met by the form of one weary and sad,"

which the Greeks call—

> "Engonasis, because it moves with bended knees;
> And near it is placed the crown of surpassing brightness."

This is behind him; but near his head stands Anguitenens;

> "Whom the Greeks call by the celebrated name, Ophiuchus.
> He firmly grasps the snake with both his hands,
> And is, himself, enfolded by its coiled body;

> For the snake clasps the man round beneath the breast;
> But, as he walks, he plants his heavy steps,
> And treads with his feet on Nepa's breast and eyes."

The Septemtriones are, in their turn, followed by—

> '" Arctophylax, said commonly to be Bootes,
> Because he drives before him the Bear yoked to a pole."

After him those that follow; for this Bootes has

> '" Around his waist, a star of glittering rays;
> Arcturus of distinguished name,"—

and beneath his feet moves on

> '" The Virgo of brilliant form, holding a shining spike."

43. 'And all those constellations are so clearly defined that in the whole diagram the design of a God is evident.

> '" The Gemini you will descry close by the Bear's head
> Beneath his breast is Cancer; and by his feet is held
> The mighty Leo darting from his body a quivering flame."

Auriga

> '" On the left side of the Gemini will move,
> His forehead the fierce Helice defends
> While Capra occupies his left shoulder."

Then come the following:

> '" But this is distinguished by a great and glorious constellation:
> The Hædi, on the other side, cast but a faint light on mortals;"

and beneath his feet

> '" The horned Taurus with his strong frame is placed."

His head is studded with thickly sown stars,

> '" These the Greeks commonly call Hyades,"

from raining; for *huein* means "to rain:" though our people ignorantly call them *Suculæ*, as if they took their name from that of swine, instead of the rain. Cepheus, next, follows the smaller Septemtrio behind, with extended hands,

> '" For Cynosura revolves close by the Bear's back."

He is preceded by

'"Cassiopea with a feeble gleam of stars,
While near her moves with glittering body
Andromeda, sadly avoiding the presence of her parents.
The Horse, tossing his mane of gleaming light,
Touches her head; and one star uniting them,
Holds the two figures in its twofold light,
Wishing to tie an eternal knot of stars,
Then close comes Aries with his curling horns."

Near him are :

'"The Fishes, of whom one seems in haste,
Somewhat before the other, to the force
Of the North wind exposed."

44. 'At the feet of Andromeda Perseus appears on the map—

'"And him the sharp blasts of the North winds beat.
Near his left knee, though dim their light,
You will perceive the little Pleiades, and find,
Not far from them, the Lyre but slightly joined.
Next comes the winged bird, that seems to fly
Beneath the spacious canopy of sky."

Nearest to the Horse's head is the right hand of Aquarius, and then his whole form.

'"Then Capricorn, with half the shape of beast,
Breathes chill and piercing cold from his strong breast;
And, in a spacious circle moves around,
When him, while in the winter solstice bound,
The sun has visited with constant light,
He turns again and shorter makes the night."

He in turn becomes visible.

'"The Scorpion rising upward on his course.
Near him the Archer with his bended bow.
Near him the bird with brilliant plumage spread,
And the fierce eagle hovers o'er his head."

Then the Dolphin,

'"Climbing diagonally with all his frame;"

And following him,

'"The blazing Dog-star glows with starry light."

Next, the Hare follows—

' " Unwearied in his course—at the Dog's tail,
Argo moves on, and moving seems to sail.
Above, the Ram and Fishes have their place,
The famous vessel touches in her pace
The River's bank."

Which, winding and flowing far, you will perceive,

' " The fetters at the Fishes' tail are hung.
By Nepa's head, behold the Altar stand,
Which by the South wind's gentle breath is fann'd ;"

and close by, the Centaur,

' " Hastens his equine limbs to join beneath
The Serpent; then, extending his right hand,
To where you see the Monster Scorpion stand,
Which he at the bright altar fiercely slays.
Here on her tail the Hydra stands erect."

Her body trails a long distance,

' " And in her middle coils the bright Cratera shines.
Her end, Corvus rising with plumed body strikes
With beak, and stands close underneath the Twins ;
Before the Dog, called Procyon in Greek."

Can any sane man suppose that all this diagram of stars, and all this vast garniture of heaven, could have resulted from the accidental and unguided movements of matter? Or, in fact, could any physical principle, destitute of intellect and reason, have produced all this, which not only required intelligence for its production, but cannot even be understood without a high order of intellect?

45. 'Nor, indeed, are these facts alone wonderful; but, there is none grander than this ; that the globe is so solid, and holds together for stability in such a way that nothing more suited to its purpose can be even imagined ; for all its parts, everywhere gravitating to the centre, exert an equal pressure. But masses of matter joined together are most permanent when enclosed and kept together by something equivalent to a chain; and this is what is done by that physical principle which accomplishes everything by intelligence and reason, pervades the whole system, and forces and directs the distant parts to the centre. For this reason, if the universe is circular, so that all its parts are evenly

attracted by each other; the same force must affect the earth, so that, with all its parts gravitating to the centre—and that centre is the lowest point in the globe—nothing can interpose by which such a force of gravitation and weight could be counteracted.

'On the same principle, the sea, though it lies on the earth, yet, gravitating to the centre, is evenly massed everywhere, and never passes its limit or overflows. The air, however, in contact with this, tends upwards by its lightness, and yet diffuses itself everywhere; so that, although in unbroken contact with the sea, it has an intrinsic tendency to the sky; and modified by its rarity and heat, yields vital and healthy breath to animals. Encircling this, the highest region of the sky, called the æthereal, retains its own heat, gaseous and unmixed, and is at the same time in contact with the highest stratum of the air.

46. 'Again, in the æther the stars revolve, and being globular, keep their places by their own gravity, and maintain their motion by their mere shape and form; because they are round, and to that shape—as I believe I said before—there is least possibility of injury. The stars are also of a fiery nature; and, for that reason, are fed by those exhalations from earth and sea and rivers, which are drawn up by the sun from land and water when heated; and fed and refreshed by these, the stars and the whole æther give back the same substance and again attract it at intervals; so that the loss is almost nothing or very little that the fire of the stars and æther consumes. And from this our sect believe—what it is said that Panætius doubted—that it will eventually happen that the whole universe will take fire, when, on the exhaustion of moisture, neither the land can receive nourishment, nor the air be replaced, for, it cannot be produced when all the water is used up; and so, nothing would be left but fire; from the reviving of which and the Deity a renewal of the universe would ensue, and the original arrangement be restored. I am unwilling to be tedious in my account of the stars, and of those especially that are called planets; but, such is their harmony in their several movements that, while the most distant star of Saturn is freezing, and that of Mars in the centre is glowing; and between these Jupiter is brilliant and cool, and the two inside Mars are exposed to the sun; the sun itself fills the whole system with light, and the moon, illumined by him, presides over

pregnancy and births and brings them to maturity; and whomsoever this combination of action and—so to speak—co-operation of nature does not convince, has never, I am quite sure, reflected upon any of those facts.

47. 'Well, then—to pass on from astronomic questions to those of earth—What is there in these in which the design of an intellectual essence is not manifest? In the first place, the stems of all that grows from the earth give stability to those that are supported by and draw from the ground the sap by which all those are nourished that are held by roots, and are clothed with inner and outer bark, to protect them from cold and heat. Vines, also, take hold of their supports with tendrils, as with hands, and climb like living things, and still more, they are said to shrink from cabbages, if planted near them, as if they were noxious and poisonous, and never to touch them.

'Of animals, what a variety there is! and how strong a tendency to this object, that they may continue in their several species! Of these, some are protected by hides; some clothed in fur: some bristling with quills; others we see covered with feathers; and others with scales; some armed with horns; and others having the resource of wings. Nature has, also, provided in abundance the food suited to each. I could recount how ingenious and delicate is the arrangement of organs in the anatomy of animals, for taking and digesting that food; and how wonderful is the mechanism of limbs; for, all the internal organs are so formed and placed, that there is nothing superfluous in them; nothing that is not indispensable to the maintenance of life. The same Nature has given to lower animals perception and appetite; so that through the one they may be inclined to seize their congenial food, and by the other, distinguish wholesome from poisonous substances. Still further, some animals reach their food by walking, some by crawling, some by flying, and others by swimming; and seize it, some with open mouth and teeth, some with the gripe of talons, some with hooked beaks; some live by suction, some by grazing, some by devouring, and some by chewing. The position of some is so low, that they can easily reach their ground food with their snouts; while such as are taller—geese, swans, cranes and camels—are assisted by the length of their necks. To the elephant even a hand has been given, because, by reason of his size, he finds access to his food difficult.

48. 'But, to those animals whose food is such that they live upon animals of other species, Nature has given strength or speed: on some even a degree of mechanical craft has been bestowed; so that some weave a sort of net of cobwebs, in order to kill whatever falls into it. Others keep watch, as if inadvertently, and seize and devour what comes in their way. The *pinna* (naker), for instance—for so it is called in Greek—formed of two large flat shells, enters into a sort of partnership with the little shrimp, for obtaining food; and, accordingly, when small fishes swim into the open shells, the naker, warned by the shrimp, closes the shells. Thus, food is sought in company by animals widely different; and in this, the wonder is, whether they are brought into combination by any mutual understanding, or by an inborn instinct.

'There is, also, some cause for wonder in those aquatic animals that are born on land; as crocodiles and river tortoises and some snakes, born out of the water, run to it as soon as they are able to move. Still further, we sometimes place duck's eggs under hens, from which when the young birds are born, they are fed by them as mothers by whom they have been hatched into life. Afterwards they leave them and evade their pursuit, as soon as they get sight of the water which may be called their natural element.

49. 'I have also seen it stated of a bird named *platalea* (the spoonbill), that it procures its food by flying at other birds that dive in the sea; and when these come to the surface, after catching a fish, biting them on the head, until they let go what they have caught, and then seizing it for itself. This same bird is described as filling itself with shell-fish, and when it has stewed them by the heat of its stomach, disgorging them, and picking out what is eatable.

'Frog-fishes, too, are said to be in the habit of covering themselves with sand, and crawling by the water side, and when fishes approach them, as so much food, they are killed and eaten by the frogs.

'The hawk maintains a sort of natural warfare with the raven; so that each breaks the eggs of the other wherever it finds them. From this discovery of Aristotle, who made many others, who can withhold his admiration?

'When cranes cross the sea in search of a warmer climate, they form a triangle: by its apex the resistance of the air is diverted from them; and then, imperceptibly, by the wings on both sides, as by oars, the flight of the birds is assisted:

the base of the triangle which they form is impelled as if by a following wind; while those behind lay their necks and heads on the backs of those flying in front; and, as the leader himself cannot do this, having nothing to lean upon, he flies to the rear to take rest: his place is taken by one of those who have rested; and that succession is kept up through the whole journey. I could mention many other facts of the same kind; but you see the general principle. It is still better known how carefully animals look to their safety, how they look around when feeding, and conceal themselves in their lairs.

50. 'In fact, all such things are wonderful. What can I say of the discoveries made recently—that is, a few centuries ago—by the skill of physicians? Dogs relieve their stomachs by emetics; and the Ægyptian ibis by purgation. It is said that panthers which used, in wild countries, to be caught by means of poisoned meat, have a remedy by the use of which they escape death; and that, in Crete, wild goats, when wounded by poisoned arrows, resort to a herb called dittany, by tasting which they say that the arrows drop out of their flesh: stags, also, immediately before giving birth, cleanse themselves thoroughly with a herb called *seseli* (castor oil).

'We see, in other instances, how they defend themselves with their several weapons against violence and alarm—bulls with their horns, boars with tusks, lions with teeth; others save themselves by speed; others by concealment; the cuttle-fish by effusion of ink; the torpedo by an electric shock; and some, also, keep off pursuers by a smell of intolerable nastiness.

51. 'But, in order that the garniture of the globe may be maintained, special care has been taken by the providence of the Gods that there shall always be various kinds of animals and trees and all else that are held in the ground by their stems: and all these contain such a quantity of seed, that many are produced from one; and that seed is enclosed in the inmost part of the berries that issue from the stem; and by these seeds men are abundantly fed, and the ground is supplied by the renewal of plants of the same kind.

'Why need I allude to the evident instinct of all animals, in the perpetuation of their kind? In the first place, some are male and some female, as nature has arranged for their continuance. When the young animal is born, nearly all the food of the mother, in the case of those that are fed with milk, begins to assume that form, and the animals only just born, untaught and guided by instinct, resort to the teats, and from their abundance satisfy themselves.

'And, that we may perceive that, in all this, nothing is accidental, and that it is the work of a wise and provident being—to those which produce manifold offspring, such as swine and dogs, a number of teats is given, while the animals that produce few have few in proportion. Why need I mention how strong the affection of animals is in rearing and guarding their offspring, until that period when they can protect themselves? Fishes, however, they say, forsake their eggs, when they produce them; because they are easily preserved, and are fertilized in the water.

52. 'It is said that, on the other hand, tortoises and crocodiles, after producing their offspring on land, bury their eggs and go away; so that they are born and reared without help. Domestic and other birds require not only a quiet place for hatching, but construct beds and nests for themselves, and line them as softly as they can, so that their eggs may be most easily protected; and when they bring out their chickens, guard them so carefully that they shelter them with their wings, lest they should suffer from the cold; and, if the sun shines, interpose their own bodies. But, when the young birds are able to use their wings, then the mothers accompany their flight and are relieved from further trouble.

'For the preservation and health of some animals and products of the soil, human skill and diligence are contributed. There are, in fact, many animals and plants that cannot thrive without the care of man. Ample facilities also, are found severally in different places for human cultivation and abundance. The Nile waters Ægypt, and, after keeping it submerged and flooded all the summer, retires and leaves the fields softened and top-dressed for planting. The Euphrates fertilizes Mesopotamia, into which it may be said to bring fresh soil every year. But, the Indus, which is the largest of all rivers, not only enriches and reclaims the soil, but even plants it; for it is said to bring down with it large quantities of seed resembling corn. I could mention many other memorable facts peculiar to different places, and many varieties of soil rich in their respective crops.

53. 'But, how great is the generosity of nature in this, that it produces so many and different and enjoyable materials

for food, and not merely at one season of the year, so that we are always regaled by their novelty and abundance! How seasonable and beneficial, not to mankind only, but to cattle, and in fact, to all that grows from the earth, is the gift of the Etesian winds by whose breath excessive heat is moderated! By these, also, the mariner's course is guided with speed and certainty. Many facts must be omitted, and yet there are many to be mentioned.

'It would be impossible to recount the conveniences of rivers, the alternate ebb and flow of the tides; the mountains clad with forests; salt mines at long distances from the sea coast; the earth prolific in healing medicines; and, in short, sciences without number, indispensable to sustenance and life. The alternation, also, of day and night preserves animals by marking out different intervals of action and repose.

'Thus it is, on all sides and by every argument, proved that all things in this world are wonderfully ordered for the safety and preservation of all.

'But, if one inquires, For whose sake the structure of so great a world has been made? Is it for trees and herbs?—for these, though destitute of perception, are still supported by nature—that would be absurd. Is it, then, for the lower animals? It is not more likely that the Gods have taken so much trouble for the sake of dumb and unintelligent creatures. For whom, then, should one say that the world has been created? Of course, for those living beings who enjoy reason. These are Gods and men, than whom there is certainly nothing higher; for it is reason that excels everything; and so, it becomes easy to believe that, for the sake of Gods and men, the world and all that it contains were made.

54. 'It will be more easily understood that provision has been made for men by the immortal Gods, if the whole human organization is reviewed, and all the mechanism and completeness of man; for, as the life of all animals depends on three things—food, drink, and air; the mouth, assisted in breathing by the nose, is specially suited to the reception of all these. By teeth set in the mouth, food is grasped and by them broken up and softened. Those in front, being sharp, break the food by biting it. The back, called jaw-teeth, masticate it; and this process is apparently assisted by the tongue. The throat, into which the contents of the

mouth fall, connected with its roots, comes next to the tongue: this, reaching to the tonsils on both sides, is terminated by the inner edge of the palate; and when it receives the food driven, and in a manner forced down by the action and motion of the tongue, it sends it on; while that section of it below the food expands, and that above is contracted. But, as the rough artery—the trachea—for so it is called by physicians—has an aperture attached to the root of the tongue, a short distance above the connection of the throat with it; and as, extending to the lungs, it conveys the air received in breathing, it is protected by a valve with which it is furnished, for this purpose, that, in case any food should fall upon it, the breath may not be stopped. But, as the stomach, placed below the throat, is the receptacle of food and drink; while the lungs and heart receive air from without, the stomach, which consists principally of nerves, exhibits many wonderful contrivances; for it is complicated and tortuous, and clasps and holds what it receives—whether dry or fluid—so that it can be transformed and digested, and is alternately contracted and expanded, and compresses and mixes what it receives; so that by the heat of which it has a high degree, and by grinding the food, and still further, by the air, it is all dressed and liquefied, and distributed to the rest of the body.

55. 'The lungs, again, have an open texture and spongy softness, specially suited to inhaling the breath; as they contract and expand in inhaling; so that the food of life by which animals are principally sustained, is frequently drawn in. From the stomach, the fluid by which we are nourished, separated from the rest of the food, flows through some direct passages, to the tubes of the liver—as they are called—belonging to and connected with it: and then, there are other connecting tubes, through which the food descends, when discharged from the liver. When from that food the bile and the liquid flowing from the kidneys are secreted, the rest is converted into blood, and flows to the same ducts of the liver to which all its passages lead. Passing through these, it is there poured into the vein called *cava*, and through that, refined and liquefied, to the heart; and from that, by a numerous network of veins, to all parts of the body. How the refuse of the food is removed by the alternate compression and expansion of the intestines, would be easily described, but must be omitted; so that my speech may involve nothing

disagreeable. Let me rather describe the rest of the wonderful mechanism of nature.

'The air drawn into the lungs by breathing is warmed, first by the nose in the act of inhaling, and then by contact with the lungs; after which, some is exhaled, and the rest admitted into that part of the heart called the ventricle, to which another similar one is attached, into which the blood flows from the liver through the *cava* vein. In that way the blood is, from these organs, propelled through the whole body; and air through the arteries: and both these systems, closely and numerously interwoven all through the body, attest an inconceivable faculty of ingenious and superhuman contrivance.

'What shall I say of the bones, which, as the frame of the body, have joints wonderfully designed for strength, and conveniently terminating the limbs, for motion and every action of the body? Add to this the nerves by which the limbs are controlled and their reticulation through the whole frame: for these—like the veins and arteries, proceeding from the heart—are distributed all over the body.

56. 'To this providence of Nature, so careful and ingenious, many details could be added, from which it may be inferred, what large and valuable privileges have been given to man by the Gods. It is this providence that formed men, when first called into life from the earth, erect, so that, by looking upon the heavens, they might acquire a knowledge of the Gods. Men are of the earth, not as visitors or inhabitants, but, in some measure, spectators of high and heavenly objects, the view of which is given to no other animal. The organs of sense, in their turn, the interpreters and reporters of their several objects, are admirably placed in the head, as a citadel, and formed for their indispensable uses; for the eyes, as if on the look-out, occupy the highest position, from which, by commanding the widest view, they may perform their duty; and the ears, as they have to take notice of sound, which naturally tends upwards, are properly set in a high position. The nose, also, as all odours have an upward tendency, is suitably allotted a high place; and, having an acute perception of food and drink, has, not without reason, sought the neighbourhood of the mouth. The sense of taste, which performs the function of distinguishing the properties of what we eat, has a place in that part of the mouth where Nature has made a passage for food and drink. The sense of

touch is evenly distributed over the whole body : so that we may be able to feel every impact and every slightest incident of cold and heat : and, as, in buildings, architects remove from the sight and smell of the owners everything that would, if exposed to view, be certain to excite some disgust ; so has Nature removed objects of the same kind from the organs of sense.

57. 'What mechanic but Nature—than which no other can be more skilful—could have displayed so much ingenuity in the organs of sense? For, it has, in the first place, clothed and protected the eyes with most delicate membranes; and these it has made transparent, so that light may pass through, and sufficiently strong to confine them; while it has lubricated the eyes and made them moveable ; so that they shrink aside from whatever might hurt them, and easily turn their view in any direction they please : and the lens itself, which is called the pupil, is so small that it can easily avoid whatever might injure it ; while the lids, which cover the eyes, soft as possible to the touch, so as not to hurt the lens, are most suitably formed for enclosing and exposing the pupils, lest anything should touch them : and this also it has provided, that this movement can be made at intervals with the utmost rapidity. The lids are furnished with a sort of palisade of hairs, by which any external object can be repelled from the eyes, when open or closed in sleep, when we do not use them for seeing, so that they can repose under cover. Still further, they are conveniently set back, and defended by the prominence of the surrounding parts; for, in the first place, the upper edge, covered with eyebrows, keeps off the sweat running from the head and brow : secondly, the cheeks, slightly projecting beneath, are a protection below ; and the nose is so placed that it seems like a wall standing between them. The ears, on the contrary, are always open ; for we require their perception even while asleep, and when sound strikes on them we are awakened. They have a tortuous entrance, to prevent the intrusion of anything that might enter, if the avenue were straight and direct ; and it is further provided that, if even the smallest animal should attempt an entrance, it would be clogged by the secretion of the ear, as by birdlime. The external ear, so called, is formed for covering and protecting the organ, and preventing the sound which strikes it from escaping and being lost, before reaching it ; while it has rigid and horny avenues,

with many convolutions; because sound is increased by the reverberation of those contrivances. On the same principle, in stringed instruments, reverberation is produced by shell or horn, and a louder tone is given back from the tortuous and hollow space.

'In like manner, the nostrils which, for their indispensable uses, are always open, have narrow entrances, to prevent anything that might be injurious from passing through, and are always supplied with moisture, useful in excluding dust and other substances. The organ of taste is well protected, being enclosed in the mouth, for its use and the insurance of its safety: and all the human senses are much more perfect than those of lower animals.

58. 'In the first place, for instance, the eyes exercise a high faculty of criticism in those arts, the estimation of which is their peculiar function—in painting, sculpture, and embossing, as well as in the gesture and attitude of the body. The eye is, also, the judge of the beauty and symmetry of colour and form, and—so to say—of gracefulness, and many other objects; for it can distinguish virtues and faults—anger and gentleness, joy and sorrow, courage and cowardice, assurance and timidity it can detect.

'To the ear, also, belongs a wonderful power of artistic criticism by which, in the music of the voice and of wind and stringed instruments, the changes of tone, and time, and expression, and the various qualities of voice—clear and husky, smooth and harsh, flat and sharp, flexible and rigid—are all distinguished.

'The organs of smell and taste, and, to some extent, of touch, have also a considerable power of selection. For the attraction and gratification of these senses, more arts than I could wish, have been discovered; for it is well known to what perfection the manufacture of perfumes, the seasoning of viands and sensual allurements have been brought.

59. 'And now, whoever fails to perceive that the human mind and intellect, reason, wisdom, prudence, have been brought to perfection by divine providence, seems to me to be destitute of those faculties. When discussing this topic, Cotta, I could wish for the gift of your eloquence. How ably you would treat it! What clearness—to begin with—and then, the connection of causes and consequences and the perception of that connection would be at our command; for thereby we infer logically what results from every fact, and

define and accurately include every particular, by which process it is scientifically ascertained what effect it has and what its character is—a faculty than which, not even in a God, can any other be higher. But, how important are those inferences which you of the Academy invalidate and deny— that by our senses and our reason we perceive and understand what is external! It is by the collection and comparison of such facts that we invent arts, some indispensable to the purposes of life; and some for our enjoyment. And that mistress of the world—as you usually call it—eloquence—how glorious and godlike it is! It is this, first, that enables us to learn what we know not, and to teach others what we know. Secondly, by this we encourage and persuade, and comfort the afflicted; by this we relieve the timid of their fears: we check the impatient, and mitigate desire and anger. It is this that has bound us together in a community of laws, general and special, and of cities. This has reclaimed us from wild and savage life. But, for the purpose of language, it is incredible—when one comes to think of it—what machinery Nature has contrived; for, in the first place, an air-tube extends from the lungs to the back of the mouth, through which the voice, taking its origin from the mind, is formed and uttered. Secondly, the tongue, placed in the mouth, is confined by the teeth. This shapes and articulates the informed stream of sound, and renders the tones of the voice distinct and sharp, by forcing it against the teeth and other parts of the mouth: so that our sect usually say that the tongue is analogous to a quill, the teeth to strings, and the nose to the horns which accompany string instruments in music.

60. 'But, how aptly suited to their purpose, and instrumental in how many arts, are the hands which Nature has given to man! The easy closing and opening of the fingers, by means of pliant joints and divisions, facilitates every movement; so that, the hand is adapted to painting, modelling, engraving, and producing music from wind and string instruments. And while these capabilities contribute to our amusement, the former supply our wants. I mean the cultivation of land, the erection of houses, the clothing of our bodies, either woven or seamed, and all the manufactures of copper and iron: from which it appears that by application of the mechanic's hand to the inventions of the mind, and the perception of the senses, we have realized all the advan-

tages of being sheltered, clothed, and in health; and in possession of cities, walls, houses and temples. Still further; it is by the industry—that is, the hand—of man, that variety and abundance of food are obtained. For the land yields many products acquired by the hands, to be either consumed at once, or preserved and stored for future use; while we live, also, upon animals of land and water, and birds; some by hunting and others by home-feeding.

'We secure, also, by training, the carrying power of quadrupeds, whose speed and strength are an addition to our own: we lay burdens and yokes upon some of them: we avail ourselves, for our own benefit, of the high intelligence of the elephant and the sagacity of the dog. From the depths of the earth we draw forth iron, so indispensable to agriculture: we discover deeply buried mines of copper, silver and gold, practically useful and effective in decoration: and we employ felled trees and all sorts of garden and forest timber, some for warming ourselves by application of fire and cooking our food, and some for building; that, under the shelter of a roof, we may keep off heat and cold. It further supplies large demands for building ships, by whose voyages all the necessaries of life are supplied; while of all the most violent agencies of nature—sea and wind—we alone, through our knowledge of navigation, have the control, and the use and enjoyment of the many products of the sea.

'Of the produce of the land the command belongs exclusively to man. It is we who enjoy the plain and the mountain. To us belong the rivers and the lakes: the corn and the trees are of our planting: we fertilize the land by irrigation: we confine, guide and divert the current of the river: with our hands, in short, we endeavour to create a sort of second nature in the physical world.

61. 'What can I say more? Has not human intellect found its way even into the heavens? For, we alone of all animals have studied the rising, setting and orbits of the stars. By mankind the day, the month, and the year have been measured: and eclipses of the sun and moon ascertained and foretold for all future time—their identity, their extent and their dates.

'From the contemplation of these facts comes piety, with which justice and other virtues are associated; and from these results a happy life, resembling in kind and degree that of the Gods, inferior in nothing but immortality, which is not a necessary condition of happiness.

'By the statement of these proofs, I believe I have fully shown how far human nature surpasses all other animals; and from this it should be inferred that neither the form nor the position of our limbs, nor our mental faculties, could be what they are by accident. It now remains for me to conclude by proving that all the contents of this world, which man uses, are prepared and created for his sake.

62. 'In the first place, the globe itself has been created for Gods and men, and all that it contains is intended and designed for man's benefit. The globe is, in fact, a sort of home or city, the common property of Gods and men. For they alone, through the use of reason, live under general and special laws. As it is to be supposed, then, that Athens and Sparta were built for Athenians and Lacedæmonians; and, as all the wealth in those cities is properly said to belong to those nations; so, all the contents of the whole world must be supposed to belong to Gods and men. Now, the revolutions of the sun, moon, and other stars, though contributing to the harmony of the universe, do nevertheless, also, present a diorama to human eyes—there is, in fact, no exhibition more inexhaustible; none surpassing it in beauty, or, more excellent in design and ingenuity. By calculating their movements, we have learned the maturity and diversities and changes of the seasons; and, if these are known to man only, it must be concluded that they are designed for him. Does the earth, so prolific in corn and vegetables of all kinds, which it yields with the largest generosity, seem to produce all these for wild animals, or for men?

'Why need I speak of the vines and olive-gardens? For their most abundant and luxuriant produce has no relation whatever to lower animals. Quadrupeds, in fact, have no skill in planting or cultivating, or harvesting in due season, or gathering and storing crops. Of all such operations, the profit and the labour belong to man.

63. 'As it must be said, therefore, that string and wind instruments are made for those who can use them; so, must it be admitted that all those gifts which I have mentioned, are intended exclusively for those who profit by them; for we cannot say that whatever beasts may steal or take by force, has been produced for their sake also. Because men store their corn, not for rats or ants, but for their wives and

children and their own households; so that lower animals, as I said, take their enjoyment by stealth; and the owners openly and freely. It must be admitted, then, that it is for men that all this material abundance is provided; unless, perhaps, all this large supply of fruits, and not only their pleasant flavour, but their beauty and perfume, suggest a doubt that nature could have been so generous only to man.

'It is so far out of the question that this provision has been made for lower animals that we find that they have been, themselves, created for the service of man. What other purpose do sheep serve than that man clothes himself with their fleeces dressed and woven? In fact, they could neither be fed nor kept alive, nor yield any profit, without the management and care of man. But the trusty vigilance of the dog and his affectionate devotion to his master, his jealousy of strangers, his inconceivable keenness of scent in searching and his activity in hunting—what do they imply, but that they have been brought into existence for the convenience of man?

'What can I say of oxen? For their backs show, of themselves, that they are not formed for bearing loads; while their necks were made for the yoke, and the strength and breadth of their shoulders for drawing the plough. To these, when the ground was pulverized by the partition of the clods, no violence was ever offered—as poets tell—by the men of the happy age of gold.

'"But suddenly, an age of iron followed,
And ventured first to forge the deadly sword,
And eat the ox fettered and tamed by force."

So valuable was the service supposed to be rendered by oxen, that it was considered a crime to eat their flesh.

64. 'It would be tedious to enumerate the services of mules and asses, which have certainly been intended for man. But, what can the hog supply except food? Chrysippus, indeed, says that life is given to it, as so much salt, to prevent decomposition. Anything more prolific than this animal, because it is adapted for human food, nature has not produced.

'Why need I mention the number and flavour of fishes and of birds? From these so much enjoyment is derived, that the Pronœa of our creed may sometimes appear to have been Epicurean; and these could not be even caught, except by the intelligence and ingenuity of men; though we believe that some birds—flappers and screamers, as our augurs call them—have been created for purposes of divination. Still further, we obtain savage wild beasts by hunting; to eat them, and at the same time train ourselves, while pursuing them, to a semblance of military discipline, and employ them when tamed and educated, as we use elephants; and extract from their bodies many remedies for diseases and wounds, as we do from some plants and herbs, the virtues of which we have learned from long practice and experiments.

'We can survey in imagination, as with our eyes, all lands and seas—you will see fruitful districts, immeasurable plains, the thick foliage of the mountains, feeding ground for flocks, and inconceivably rapid currents of the sea; and it is not only on the surface of the earth, but in its deepest recesses that many useful objects are concealed, which were created for and are discovered by man alone.

65. 'But that fact, which you both will, probably, take hold of for your censure—Cotta, because Carneades took pleasure in assailing the Stoics; and Velleius, because there is nothing that Epicurus treats with so much ridicule as prophecy of coming events—seems to me the very strongest proof that human interests are guarded by divine providence. For divination certainly is a fact, which shows itself in many places and events, and on occasions of personal and especially of national importance. The inspectors of victims see much; augurs evince much foresight; many revelations are made by oracles; many by dreams and by portents; through the knowledge of which human interests are secured by wisdom and expediency, and many dangers averted. This, therefore, whether a science or an intuition, has been given by the Gods to man, and to no other being for the knowledge of future events; and, if particular instances of this do not influence you; at least, all taken together in their intimate association must have some effect: because it is not only for the whole human race, but for individuals also, that thought is habitually taken and provision made by the immortal Gods; for we can regard the human race collectively, and reduce it gradually to a comparatively few, and eventually to individuals.

66. 'Because, if we believe, for the reasons I have already stated, that the Gods take thought for all men everywhere, in whatever part of the universe, separated from all connec-

tion with this land which we inhabit: they take an interest in those, also, who inhabit this land with us, from East to West. And if, again, they take thought for those who inhabit what may be considered a large island; they take care of those, also, who occupy the divisions of that island— Europe, Asia, Africa; they, therefore, give their attention even to subdivisions of these; such as Rome, Athens, Sparta, Rhodes, and to individuals in these cities, separately from the general mass; as our nation and Greece produced Curius, Fabricius and Coruncanius, in the war with Pyrrhus; in the first Punic war, Calatinus, Duillius, Metellus and Lutatius; in the second, Maximus, Marcellus, Africanus; after these, Paullus, Gracchus and Cato; and in the time of our fathers, Scipio, Lælius, and many eminent men besides, none of whom can be supposed to have been what he was without divine assistance: and this consideration induced the poets, and notably Homer, to associate certain Gods with their principal heroes—Ulysses, Diomed, Agamemnon, Achilles— as comrades in difficulties and dangers. Still further, the personal visits of Gods, such as I mentioned above, proclaim their interest in the affairs of nations and individuals; which is to be inferred, also, from intimations of coming events which are given to us asleep and awake. We receive many warnings from sacrifices, also, and omens and many other appearances, which daily experience has so recorded, as to make divination a science. No man, therefore, has ever been great without some divine inspiration: nor is the fact to be negatived by supposing that, if the weather injures any man's corn or vineyards, or, if an accident deprives him of any of the comforts of life, the person to whom anything of the kind happens, is hated or neglected by God. The Gods attend to large and overlook small interests. With great men, however, everything always turns out fortunately; since enough has been said by our sect, and by Socrates, the first of philosophers, concerning the richness and resources of virtue.

67. 'This is very nearly what occurred to me, of what I thought might be said respecting the nature of Gods. You, however, Cotta, if you listen to my advice, would take the same side, and remember that you are a leading citizen and a priest: and, as your sect are free to defend either side, choose this in preference, and devote to this purpose that power of argument which you acquired from your rhetorical

exercises, and the Academy improved; for the habit of arguing against the Gods, either sincerely or ostensibly, is perverse and impious.'

NOTES.

Ch. 2. Though the arguments stated in this and the two following chapters are not by any means what might be expected from the champion of a school who negatived every theory of the Epicureans, still, he arrives at the same conclusion in recognising the infallibility of a universal and uniform intuition; though it could derive no logical support from the traditions which he repeats, except so far as such legends, however intrinsically absurd, may prove the existence of the intuition on which they are founded.

Ch. 2. *Apud Regillum.* Parallels to this miraculous legend of the Dioscuri are to be found in the histories of several other nations—notably, in that period of the history of Spain which records the exploits of the Cid. Even the early history of Christianity supplies evidence of the same pervading superstition. Describing an engagement which took place during the siege of Antioch, in the first Crusade, A.D. 1098, Gibbon writes: 'Three knights, in white garments and resplendent armour, either issued, or seemed to issue, from the hills: the voice of Adhemar, the Pope's legate, proclaimed them as the martyrs, St. George, St. Theodore, and St. Maurice. The tumult of battle allowed no time for doubt or scrutiny; and the welcome apparition dazzled the eyes or the imagination of a fanatic army.'

Ch. 4. *At fortasse.* This is an obviously false analogy; because medicine is a human and, to some extent, experimental science; while the faculty of prophecy is supposed to be of divine origin, and is nothing, therefore, if not infallible; and if signs are misinterpreted, it is because they are not sufficiently plain and legible.

Ch. 8. The argument stated in these curious syllogisms is ingeniously, but, at the same time, transparently sophistical. The logical defects are, in the first place, the inference of an affirmative conclusion from premises of which one is negative, which involves the violation of a general rule. But, secondly, even if this anomaly is obviated by the substitution of an equivalent affirmative for the negative premiss, the argument would still have the appearance of being inverted, which it really is, being in one of those indirect moods of the first figure, which were eventually—by Galen, in the second century—classified as a fourth figure. Thirdly, the great defect is that each of the syllogisms really contains two perfectly distinct middle terms. In one premiss, 'better' means 'higher in the order of being'; in the other, it signifies 'materially or physically superior': if not, then the minor premiss is obviously false; any animal—as Cotta, *i.e.*, Cicero says—being of a higher order than the material globe. His main refutation, however, is the elaborate *reductio ad impossible* in 3, 9. A rational being, says the syllogism, is better, *i.e.*, of a higher order, than any unintelligent aggregate of matter; but the excellence of the kosmos is described as being merely material, and supplies no ground for the conclusion. Its excellence should be an inference from the possession of intellect, if that were first proved ; but it cannot possibly follow from its physical excellence that it must be an intelligent being ; because the vital and sentient faculties and other phenomena of animal life most certainly emanate from an external and spiritual source.

The analogy of musical instruments growing on trees is false, and proves nothing ; because such instruments are made every day by persons possessing no musical perception or faculty whatever ; and, so far as it relates to the kosmos, it would be just as rational to maintain that a tree is a being of a higher order than the mechanic who constructs some useful article out of the timber.

Ch. 20. *Maximé vero sunt admirabiles*, etc. The proofs of design, adduced in this and the following chapters, coincide as nearly as possible with known modern inferences, and derive an interest not only from their logical force, but from the information which they supply respecting the knowledge attained by men of that day of those physical sciences that had, in later times, altogether died out under the influences of barbarism and superstition. Beginning with the most sublime and fascinating of all sciences, the representative of the Stoics describes the several planets of the solar system according to the theory of Pythagoras, which, even without the aid of the telescope, came very much nearer to the truth than the speculations of Tycho Brahe and others of that time.

That the five planets, then identified, were globes revolving round the earth as a common centre, at different distances and in proportionate periods of time, and held in their places by gravitation, was the astronomic theory of the learned ancients, who had also, by observation of their apparent motions, marked the essential difference between planets and fixed stars. The error in transposing Venus and Mercury arose, of course, from their mistake respecting the centre of the system. The whole theory, in fact, coincided as nearly as possible with what we know as the Ptolemaic ; while their diagrams of the fixed stars were identical with those in Flamsteed's 'Atlas Cœlestis.'

The nearest approach to a telescope known to the ancients, was a long tube which made stars visible in daylight, and proved that they are something more than lamps lighted up every evening for the embellishment of our planet, and, most probably, worlds like our own : and had they only discovered the magnifying and approximating powers of lenses, it is tolerably certain that they would have left nothing for modern astronomers to discover ; while, on the other hand, if those aids to observation were still unknown, it may be a question whether the science would have advanced beyond the point to which they brought it ; because we know that, in the dark ages of European history, it reverted to the stage where optical illusions were regarded as real phenomena.

Ch. 23. *Res ipsa in qua vis inest*, etc. In this account of the intuitive human tendency to Platonic realism—*i.e.*, the personification and deification of abstract ideas—some deficiency of logical precision may be detected. From a comparison of the several sentences, it would appear that *res ipsa* and *vis* must be one and the same abstraction ; for it is impossible to draw any line of distinction applicable to all the instances ; the *vis*, or quality, being, itself, the idea, concerning the reality of which realists and nominalists have maintained the controversy originated by Plato and Aristotle.

Ch. 27. From these specimens of etymology which are of the same class with what we find in Plato's 'Cratylus,' Varro, and Ovid's 'Fasti'—we must infer—however presumptuous the inference may seem—that the ancients knew very little of the philology of the languages which they have immortalized. When we recollect, however, that they knew no other languages to compare with their own, and had no acquaintance with their original sources, we must naturally attribute their ignorance to want of opportunity. Before the discovery, or revival, of Sanskrit, our Greek and Latin lexicons exhibited the same absurdities; and—strange to say—even more recently, we find, in the Homeric studies of an eminent statesman, repetitions of long-exploded derivations, not more rational than those in which Velleius is said by Cotta *quod miserandum sit laborare.*

Ch. 28. Here Balbus anticipates and answers some of the strongest of Cotta's objections—3, 24, etc.—which are, therefore, gratuitous; especially his tiresome and repeated enumeration of all the names in the mythology. He illustrates the wide difference between religion and superstition, and eliminates from the consideration of philosophers all the absurdities of vulgar credulity; showing that the personification and canonization of abstract ideas is merely the poetical expression of a sentiment which we know to be common to all languages and a favourite embellishment with many poets—the authors, for instance, of the 'Divina Commedia,' the 'Faery Queen,' 'Paradise Lost,' the 'Pilgrim's Progress,' 'Psyche,' and many others, who were as far as possible—as far as the Greek or any other philosophers—from believing in polytheism.

Cotta's argument, being obviously based on the difficulty of drawing any line of demarcation, of course, takes the form of sorites; but, when he regards the worship of Bacchus and Ceres and the apotheosis of heroes as irrational, it would be interesting to know what an ancient philosopher would have thought of the dogma of transubstantiation and the canonization of saints.

Ch. 37. *Formæ literarum.* With respect to this curious illustration of the argument for design in creation, it seems wonderful that it did not at once lead to the invention of printing, describing, as it does, the operation technically called 'composing' type. Independently of this, it is strange that men who had got so far as branding-irons and stencil-plates, had not advanced the rest of the way.

It is, of course, scarcely necessary to observe that the twenty-one letters mentioned in the text, constituted the Latin alphabet, before the addition of zeta, kappa, and upsilon, borrowed from the Greek.

BOOK III.

1. WHEN Balbus had spoken thus, Cotta, with a smile answered: 'It is too late, Balbus, to suggest to me my line of defence; for, while you were arguing, I was considering what I should say in reply; and not so much for the purpose of refutation as of asking for information about what I failed to understand; and, as every man must use his own judgment, it is difficult for me to shape my thoughts according to your wishes.'

Here Velleius said: 'You don't know with what curiosity I am waiting to hear you; for your discourse against Epicurus was interesting to our friend Balbus; I will promise you, therefore, in turn, an attentive listener against the Stoics; for I hope you come, as usual, well prepared.' Then said Cotta: 'So I am in truth, Velleius, for I don't stand in the same relation to Lucilius as to you.' 'How is that?' said he. 'Because your Master Epicurus seems not to contend very seriously for the immortal Gods. He merely does not go so far as to deny that there are Gods, lest he should incur some odium or accusation; but, when he asserts that the Gods do nothing and care for nothing, and are furnished with human limbs, but make no use of them, he seems to be speaking in jest and to deem it sufficient to say that there is some happy and immortal being. By Balbus, on the other hand, you have observed, I suppose, how much has been said; and—though deficient in truth—how consistent and coherent. I intend, therefore, as I said, not so much to refute his speech as to seek information on what I failed to understand: so that I leave it to you, Balbus, whether you would rather answer my questions on particular points which I have not understood, or, hear my speech as a whole.'

Then said Balbus, 'I would prefer to answer you, if you want to have anything explained; but, if you wish to question me not so much for information as for refutation, I will do whichever you please—either reply at once to your separate questions, or, when you have concluded your speech, to all collectively.' 'Very good,' said Cotta; 'and so we will proceed as the discussion itself leads us.

2. 'Before I approach the subject, however, I will say a few words on my own account, for I am, in no ordinary degree, influenced by those words of yours, that, at the conclusion, advised me to bear in mind that I am Cotta, and a priest—which, I suppose, meant this: that I should uphold the doctrines which we have received from our forefathers respecting the immortal Gods, sacrifices, ceremonies and duties; I will certainly uphold and have ever upheld them, and from that belief which I have inherited, respecting the worship of the immortal Gods, no speech of either scholar or dunce shall ever draw me away; but, when religion is in question, I follow Tib. Coruncanius, P. Scipio, and P. Scævola, the high-priests, rather than Zeno, or Cleanthes or Chrysippus; and I know C. Lælius, both an augur and a philosopher, whom I would rather hear discoursing of religion in that great speech, than any leader of the Stoics: and, as all the religion of the Roman people is classified into sacrifices and divination, and a third department has been added, consisting of all that the interpreters of the Sibyl have taught us, for sake of prophecy, from signs and wonders, I have never thought that any of these observances should be discredited; and I have accepted the conviction that Romulus by auspices, and Numa by establishing worship, laid the foundations of our State, which could never have attained such greatness without the most perfect propitiation of the immortal Gods. You know, now, Balbus, what Cotta and what a priest believes. Let me know, now, what your own belief is; because from you as a philosopher I am bound to accept a system of religion, instead of believing the traditions of our ancestors.'

3. Then said Balbus, 'What system, then, do you require of me?' 'Your division,' he replied, 'was fourfold. First, you meant to prove that there are Gods; secondly, what their attributes were; thirdly, that the world is governed by them; lastly, that they provide for human interests. This, if my memory is correct, was your division.' 'Perfectly correct,' said Balbus, 'but I am waiting for your question.' Then said Cotta, 'Let us take the first separately; and since the first proposition is that which is accepted by all except utter infidels; my mind, at least, can never divest itself of the

conviction that there are Gods; and yet why that is so, of which I am convinced by the authority of former generations, you say nothing to instruct me.' 'What reason is there,' said Balbus, 'why you should wish to learn from me, if you are already convinced?' 'Because,' said Cotta, 'I am entering upon this discussion as if I had never heard anything and never thought about the immortal Gods. Take me as an ignorant and unprejudiced pupil, and teach me what I ask.' 'Say then,' said he, 'what you want.' 'I? In the first place, this—why you said so much about that very fact which you described, in your division, as not requiring discussion, because it was evident and universally accepted?' 'Because,' said he, 'I have often observed that you, too, when speaking in the forum, overwhelmed the jury with as many arguments as you could, if you only had the chance. Philosophers, also, do this; and I, to the best of my ability, have done so. When you ask that question, however, you do just as if you were to ask me why I look at you with two eyes and not with one, when I could effect the same object with one only.'

4. Then said Cotta, 'What analogy there is in that is for you to consider—for I am not in the habit of arguing, when pleading, any point that is evident and matter of universal consent; because clearness is destroyed by argument. Nor, even though I did so in law cases, would I do the same in a discussion of this critical nature. There could be no reason, however, why you should look at me with one eye, when the vision of both was the same, and when the physical law, which you maintain to be wise, provided that we should have two avenues of light from the mind to the eyes. But, as you were not sure that the fact was so evident as you wished, you chose to show us, by many arguments, that there are Gods. For me, indeed, the one fact that it is a tradition from our forefathers would be sufficient, but you discredit authority and argue by logic. Allow my logic, then, to oppose yours. You adduce all these proofs of the existence of Gods; and, to my mind, you throw a doubt, by arguing, on a fact by no means doubtful. I have, in fact, committed to memory not only the number but the order of your proofs. The first was, that when we looked up to the heavens we perceived at once that there is some divine power by which those bodies are governed. Hence, also, this quotation: " Behold this empyrean height whom all address as Jupiter;"

as if any of us would call upon that Jupiter, rather than on Capitolinus, or, as if it was self-evident and a matter of universal consent that there are Gods—though Velleius, and many others, do not admit that they are even alive. It seemed to you, also, a strong argument that a belief in immortal Gods is universal and growing stronger every day. Is it your opinion, then, that questions so important should be decided by the belief of fools—you, especially, who call them insane?

5. 'But, you say, we see Gods in person: As, for instance, Posthumius did at Lake Regillus, and Vatinius on the Salarian Road; and there is something, also, about the battle of the Locri on the Sagra. Do you, then, believe that the men whom you describe as sons of Tyndarus—that is, men born of man, whom Homer, who lived shortly after their time, describes as buried in Lacedæmon—came on white horses, and unattended, to meet Vatinius, an ignorant man, rather than bring their tidings to M. Cato, who was then in authority? In that case, do you believe, also, that the impression resembling the mark of a hoof on a stone near the Lake is of Castor's horse? Would you not rather believe what can be accepted—that the souls of distinguished men, such as those sons of Tyndarus, are deified and immortal—than that they could, when once buried, rise and take part in a battle? Or, if you say that this is possible, you ought to tell us how, and not repeat old women's stories.' Then said Lucilius, 'Do these really seem to you old women's stories? Do you not see the temple consecrated in the Forum to Castor and Pollux, and the vote of the Senate to Vatinius? So far as the Sagra is concerned, there is a popular proverb among the Greeks, who say that whatever they assert positively, is more certain than what occurred at the Sagra. Should you not, then, be influenced by such authorities?' Then said Cotta, 'You are meeting me with traditions, Balbus; but what I want is logic.' [*Here some paragraphs are lost.*]

6. 'What is to be comes after—no man can escape what is to come. Often, too, it is not even profitable to know what is coming; for it is miserable to worry one's self when one can do no good, and not have even the last and still common solace of hope; especially as you say that all events are determined by fate: and that what has been true through all eternity is fate. Of what use is it, then, or how does it help us to protect ourselves, to know any future event, as it will inevitably

come? Besides, whence comes that divination? Who discovered the partition of the liver? Who gave a meaning to the cry of the raven? Who read the sortes? For I believe all these; nor can I discredit the wand of Nævius which you mentioned. But I am bound to ascertain how they are regarded by philosophers; especially when those prophets tell so many falsehoods on sacred subjects. But physicians, also—so you said—often make mistakes. What analogy does medicine, the principle of which I can see, present to divination, the source of which I do not understand? Again, you believe that the Gods were conciliated by the martyrdom of the Decii. What prejudice of theirs was so strong, that they could not be reconciled to the Roman people unless such men had died? That was a device of commanding officers—which the Greeks call *strategema*—but such commanders as took thought for their country and cared nothing for their lives; for they expected that the army would follow a commander riding at full speed through the enemy; which actually happened. I have never heard the voice of Faunus—if you say that you have I will believe you, though I don't know at all what Faunus is.

7. 'So far, therefore, Balbus, as you are concerned, I understand nothing of the existence of Gods; and though I believe that they do exist, the Stoics teach me nothing. Cleanthes, for instance, as you said, supposes that ideas of the Gods are formed in our minds in four ways. One is that way which I have sufficiently discussed, suggested by the anticipation of future events; the second, by meteoric disturbances and other movements; the third, by the convenience and abundance of all that we enjoy; the fourth, by the arrangement and punctuality of the heavenly bodies.

'Of presentiments we have already spoken. Of meteoric, terrestrial and marine disturbances we cannot say that, when they take place, there are not many who fear them and believe that they are caused by the immortal Gods. But the question is not whether there are any who believe that Gods exist, but whether they really do exist; for the proofs that Cleanthes adduces, of which one is inferred from the abundance of the conveniences which we enjoy; the other from the succession of the seasons and the punctuality of sidereal motions, shall be considered when we take up the subject of the providence of the Gods, of which you have spoken at length. To the same opportunity we will postpone, also, the argument

—as you say that Chrysippus stated it—that, as there was something in the creation that could not be accomplished by man, there must be some power higher than man; and your comparison, also, of a decorated house with the beauty of the physical world, and your suggestion of the symmetry and harmony of the whole system, and, at the same time, all that you said scientifically about fiery action, and the heat by which you said that all things are animated, will be discussed in their proper place. And all the reasons you gave the day before yesterday—when you wanted to prove that there are Gods—why the whole globe, the sun, moon and stars, have perception and intellect, I will keep back for the same occasion. To you, however, I will put the same question again and again—by what proofs do you convince yourself that there are Gods?'

8. Then replied Balbus, 'I am certainly under the impression that I have adduced proofs; but you refute them in such a way that, when you seem to be going to ask questions, and I have prepared myself to answer, you suddenly change the subject and give me no opportunity of reply; so that the most important topics have passed unnoticed —divination, fate—questions which you touch lightly, but our school treat fully and diffusely; though they are distinct from the question now before us. Wherefore, if you please, do not confuse the discussion; so that we may obtain a clear idea of the subject of this controversy.'

'Very good,' said Cotta, 'and accordingly, as you have divided all this question into four parts, and we have disposed of the first, let us take up the second, which appears to me of such a nature that, when you meant to demonstrate the attributes of the Gods, you proved that they had no existence. You said it was very difficult to withdraw the mind from the impressions of sight; but that, as nothing was more excellent than God, you had no doubt that the globe was God; because nothing is superior to it in all creation; if only we could imagine it to be animated, or rather, see this in imagination as we see other objects with our eyes. But, when you say that nothing is superior to the globe, what do you mean by superior? If you mean more beautiful, I grant it. If you mean more suited to our requirements, I grant that also. But, if you mean superior in intelligence, I do not by any means admit it; not because it is difficult to divert the imagination from external vision,

4--3

but, because the more I do so divert it, the less able I am to conceive what you suggest.

9. 'Nothing in all the universe is superior to the globe; nor even on earth is anything superior to our city. Do you suppose, then, that, consequently, there is reason, thought, intellect in the city? or, as there is not, do you not think that an ant is, for that reason, to be classed above this fairest of cities; because there is no perceptive faculty in the city, while the ant has not only perception, but intelligence, reason, and memory? You must consider, Balbus, what is granted to you, and not assume of yourself whatever you please. In fact, that ancient and concise, and—as it seemed to you—ingenious syllogism of Zeno has given a wide scope to all that topic. Zeno argues in this form—"That which employs reason is better than that which does not: but nothing is better than the globe: therefore, the globe employs reason." If that is satisfactory, you will presently be proving that the globe must be considered the best reader of a book; because, in Zeno's formula, you can argue thus—What is learned is superior to what is not: but there is nothing superior to the globe: therefore, the globe is learned. On the same principle, the globe will be an orator, a mathematician, a musician; and, in fact, educated in all accomplishments, and, in short, a philosopher. You often said that nothing is made except by God, and that there is no power in nature to make anything unlike itself. Am I to admit that the globe is not merely animate and intelligent, but a harpist also and a trumpeter, since men of these professions spring from it? That father of the Stoics, therefore, states no reason why we should suppose that the globe enjoys reason, or is even animated. The globe is, therefore, not a God; and yet, there is nothing better; for there is nothing more beautiful, or more serviceable to us; more picturesque, more uniform in its motion. But, if the globe is not a God, neither are the stars, whose countless numbers you classed as Gods, because their regular and perpetual revolutions took your fancy; and indeed, not without reason; for they do show a wonderful and inconceivable punctuality. But it is not everything, Balbus, that shows a definite and periodical revolution, that is to be attributed to God rather than to nature.

10. 'What do you suppose could be more punctual than the Euripus of Chalkis in its alternating motion? or, than the Sicilian Strait, or the agitation of the ocean in that place

" where the rushing tide separates Europe and Libya"? Well? Cannot the tides of Spain or Britain and their ebb and flow at fixed periods take place without the agency of a God? Pray, consider; if we regard as divine all motion and everything that conforms to an arrangement of fixed periods, should it not be said, also, that tertian and quartan fevers are divine? for, what can be more punctual than the return and movement of these? But a cause has to be assigned to all such facts; and, as you cannot do that, you resort to a God as to an asylum: and in fact, Chrysippus seemed to you to speak judiciously—a man of unquestionable versatility and experience. I call those men versatile, whose minds are quick in changing their objects; and experienced, whose minds are hardened by exercise, as the hands are by work. Well, then, he says, "If there is anything that man cannot accomplish, he who can is superior to man: but man cannot create what is on the globe: he who can is, therefore, superior to man; but none can excel man but God: there is, therefore, a God." All this is involved in the same mistake with the arguments of Zeno; because it is not defined what is meant by better or more excellent, or, what the difference is between physical law and design. He says, also, that, if there are no Gods, there is nothing in all creation higher than man; and that any man should imagine that nothing is higher than man, he regards as the height of presumption. Grant that it is presumptuous to fancy one's self superior to the globe; but it is not only not presumption, but rather wisdom, to be conscious of possessing perception and reason and to know that Orion and Canicula do not possess them. He says, further, that, if a house is highly decorated, we must conclude that it was built for its owner, and not for the rats; so, therefore, we must suppose that the globe is the home of Gods. So I would certainly imagine, if I supposed it to have been built, and not, as I will prove, formed by physical laws.

11. 'But then Socrates, as reported by Xenophon, inquires whence we have got our intellect, if there was none in the globe. I ask, also, whence we derive the faculties of language, of arithmetic, of music—unless, indeed, we suppose that the sun converses with the moon, when she comes nearer, or, that the globe sings in time, as Pythagoras imagines. These are gifts of nature, Balbus—of nature not moving on mechanically, as Zeno says—and what this means we shall see presently—but giving action and motion to all things by

its own motions and transformations: and, therefore, I was pleased with those remarks respecting the harmony and co-operation of nature, which you described as acting harmoniously by a sort of unbroken affinity. I did not, however, approve your assertion that these results could not be produced unless they were controlled by one divine spirit. That system is really held together and perpetuated by the power of physical laws; not of the Gods; and involves a sort of unanimity, which the Greeks call *sympathy;* but this, in proportion as it is intrinsically stronger, has the less right to be regarded as resulting from a divine cause.

12. 'But, how do you explain away the argument that Carneades adduced?—If no body is immortal, no body can be everlasting; but no body is immortal, nor even indivisible nor incapable of separation or forcible partition; and, as every animal is constitutionally sentient, there is none that can escape the liability to receive impressions from without—that is, to endure and to suffer; and as every animal is so constituted, none is immortal. So, in like manner, as every animal can be dismembered and dissected, none of them is indivisible, none everlasting; but every animal is constituted to receive and sustain external violence, and is, therefore, mortal and decomposable and divisible. As, for instance, if all wax were transformable, there would be nothing waxen that might not be transformed; and likewise, nothing made of silver or bronze, if silver and bronze were transformable; so, on the same principle, as all existing elements of which all things consist are transformable, no body can be otherwise than liable to transformation; and, as the constituent elements of all things are transformable, according to your theory, every body is, therefore, subject to transformation. But, if any body were immortal, everything would not be transformable; and so, it is proved that all bodies are mortal: because every body is either water or air or earth or fire, or, composed of these or some portion of them; but of these there is none that is not perishable: because every earthy substance is divisible, and water is so yielding that it can be easily compressed and dashed about; fire and air are most easily moved by every impulse, and their constitution is especially yielding and dissoluble. Still further, all these perish when changed into another form, which happens when earth passes into water; and when from water air ascends, and from air æther, and they return again to their original state; so that, as those

elements perish, of which all bodies consist, no animal is everlasting.

13. 'Though we should ignore all this, still, no animal can be found that was never born and is likely to live for ever; because every animal has senses: it can, therefore, feel heat and cold, sweet and bitter; and cannot with any organ of sense receive what is pleasant and refuse to receive the opposite. So that, as it admits the sensation of pleasure, it admits pain also; and, whatever feels pain, must also experience death. It must, therefore, be granted that every animal is mortal. Still more, if there is anything that feels neither pleasure nor pain, that being cannot be an animal; and if, again, whatever is an animal must have these sensations; and whatever does experience them cannot be eternal; and if every animal feels them; then no animal can be eternal.

'Again, there can be no animal without instinctive desires and aversions: what is according to instinct is desired, the opposite is avoided; and every animal desires some things and avoids some others: what it avoids is contrary to instinct, and what is contrary to instinct has the effect of destroying life: every animal, therefore, must inevitably perish. The evidences are innumerable by which it may be proved and certified that there is nothing sentient but must die; because those very objects of sensation—for instance, heat, cold, pleasure, pain, and the rest, when intensified, are deadly; and there is no animal without sensation; therefore, no animal is everlasting.

14. 'The constitution of an animal is either single, as, for instance, of earth, or water, or air, or fire—and what this is like cannot be even imagined—or composed of several elements, each of which must have its proper place, to which it is guided by virtue of its quality—one to the highest place, another to the lowest, and another to the central. These may hold together for a time, but, by no means permanently; for each element will gravitate to its own place: therefore no animal is everlasting. But, your sect, Balbus, usually ascribe everything to fire, following Heraclitus, I believe, though not interpreting even him unanimously—but, as he was unwilling that his doctrines should be understood, let us pass them by—you say, however, that all force is fire; and therefore, that animals die when their heat is exhausted; and that, all through creation, that alone possesses life and

strength which is warm. But I cannot see how bodies should die on the exhaustion of their heat, and should not die, as well, from the loss of moisture or breath: especially when they die, also, of excessive heat. So that the doctrine of heat is two-sided. But let us look to the conclusion. Your doctrine is, I believe, that there is nothing living or sentient, in all the universe, but fire. Why so, rather than air, of which also the life of animals consists, whence the name animal? Why, again, do you take it as if for granted, that there is no life but fire? For, it seems more probable that life is a combination of fire and air. But, if fire is, in itself, an animal, without the combination of another element; as that which dwells in our bodies renders us sentient, it cannot be, itself, without sensation. The same argument can be retorted; for whatever is sentient must of course feel pleasure and pain; and to whomsoever pain comes, death must also come: and so it follows that you cannot prove even fire to be everlasting.

'Well, then—Is it not also your doctrine that all fire requires food, and it cannot in any way be permanent, unless it is fed; but that the sun, moon, and other stars are fed, some with fresh and some with salt water? Cleanthes, in fact, gives this as a reason why the sun returns and proceeds no farther, at the summer and winter solstices, lest it should go too far away from its food—what this means we shall see presently. Now, however, let this be taken as proved, that whatever is liable to death, cannot be essentially immortal; and that fire will die out if not fed: and that fire is, therefore, not essentially immortal.

15. 'But, what idea can we form of a God gifted with no virtue? What can we say? Are we to attribute to a God prudence, which consists in the knowledge of things good and bad, and neither good nor bad? What need has he of a choice between good and evil, to whom no evil ever does or can come? What need of reason? What of intelligence? Because we employ these for the purpose of attaining the unknown through the known. But, to a God nothing can be unknown. What relation to the Gods has justice, which assigns to everyone his own? For it is, as you say, human society and intercourse that created justice. Temperance, again, consists in dispensing with pleasures of the body; and, if this has a place in heaven, so have pleasures also. How can a God be supposed to exhibit fortitude in pain or hard-

ship, or danger, none of which can affect a God? How, then, can we imagine a God neither employing reason, nor gifted with any of the virtues? Nor, in fact, can I scorn the ignorance of the multitude and the uneducated, when I reflect upon what is said by the Stoics; for it is the doctrine of fools.

'The Syrians worship a fish: the Ægyptians have deified all sorts of animals: even still, they have in Greece many Gods that have been men: the Alabandi have Alabandus, the people of Tenedos Tennes. Greece in general worships Leucothea—originally Ino—and her son Palæmon, Hercules, Æsculapius, the Tyndaridæ: our people worship Romulus and many others whom they believe to be admitted into heaven, as a sort of new and naturalized denizens. Such, then, is the creed of the ignorant.

16. 'What do you philosophers say? How is your doctrine better? I pass that by, for it is notorious Grant that the globe itself is a God. This, I suppose, is that "empyrean height, whom all address as Jupiter." Why, then, do we add a number of Gods? And, what a crowd of them there is! To me they certainly do appear numerous. You reckon up the several stars, and call them either by names of beasts—as the Goat, the Scorpion, the Bull, the Lion, or, of inanimate objects—as the Argo, the Altar, the Crown. But, though all these be admitted, how can the rest be—I do not say admitted, but received at all? When we speak of corn as Ceres, and wine as Liber, we use a conventional form of language; but, do you suppose that any one is so stupid as to believe that what he eats is a God? For, as to those whom you describe as becoming Gods from being men, explain to me how that could possibly happen, or, why it ceased to happen, and I will listen with pleasure.

'As the question stands at present, I don't see how that man to whom "fire was applied on Mount Æta," as Accius says, succeeded in reaching "the eternal home of his father," from that cremation. Homer, however, represents him as met by Ulysses in the lower world, with others who had departed from life. And yet, I would like to know which Hercules we are by preference to worship; because they who search esoteric and abstruse records, recommend several to us; the most ancient being the son of Jupiter, also the most ancient; for we find several Jupiters also in the old Greek writings. Of him, then, and Lysithoe was born that Hercules who, as we have heard, contended with Apollo for a tripod. The second on record is an Ægyptian, son of Nilus, whom they mention as the author of the Phrygian books. The third is one of the Idæan Dactyli, to whom they offer funeral sacrifice. The fourth is the son of Jupiter and Asteria, sister of Latona, who is worshipped specially in Tyre, and whose daughter, they say, was Karthago. The fifth was in India, known as Belus. The sixth is this of ours, son of Jupiter and Alcmena; but Jupiter the third; because, as I will presently show, we have recognised several Jupiters also.

17. 'Since my discourse has brought me to this stage, I will prove that I have received better information respecting the worship of the immortal Gods from the Canon Law and the usage of our ancestors and from the earthen vases which Numa has left us, and Lælius mentions in that celebrated little golden speech, than from the arguments of the Stoics. Because, if I am to be led by you, tell me what answer to give to one who may ask this question—"If there are Gods, are there not also Nymphs who are Goddesses? And, if Nymphs, are there not Pans and Satyrs?" But these have no existence. Have the Nymphs, then, also no existence? But, you will say, their temples are nationally assigned and dedicated. What is the inference? Are not the others, therefore, Gods, to whom temples have been dedicated? Still further, you reckon Jupiter and Neptune as Gods; so that Orcus, their brother, is a God, and those rivers said to be in the lower world—Acheron, Cocytus, Styx, Pyriphlegethon Charon, too, and even Cerberus. But that must of course be rejected. Is not even Orcus, then, a God? What say you, then, of his brothers? This is what Carneades used to say, not for the purpose of abolishing Gods—for what could be less characteristic of a philosopher?—but to show that the Stoics have no definite ideas of them. Accordingly, he followed up the argument. What did he say? If those brothers are in the number of the Gods, can that distinction be denied to their father Saturn, whom they generally worship most in Western countries? and, if he is a God, it must be admitted that his father Cœlus is also; and, in that case, the parents of Cœlus must be regarded as Gods—Æther and Dies, and their brothers and sisters, who are named by ancient genealogists—Amor, Dolor, Metus, Labor, Invidentia, Fatum, Senectus, Mors, Tenebræ, Miseria, Querela, Gratia, Fraus, Pertinacia, the Parcæ, the Hesperides, the Somnia,

all of whom they call children of Erebus and Nox. So that, either all these unnatural objects must be admitted, or, the former excluded.

18. 'Well? Will you say that Apollo, Vulcan, Mercury, and the rest are Gods, while you hesitate respecting Hercules, Æsculapius, Liber, Castor and Pollux? But these are worshipped quite as much as the former, and by some much more. Are these, then, sons of mortal mothers, to be considered Gods? Well? Are not Aristæus, said to be the discoverer of the olive and son of Apollo, Theseus the son of Neptune, and the others whose fathers are Gods, to be included in the number? What of those whose mothers are Goddesses? Much more, I should say; because, as the child of a free mother is free, under the Civil Law; the son of a Goddess, by Natural Law, must be a God. Accordingly, the islanders of Astypalæon most devoutly worship Achilles; and, if he is a God, Orpheus and Rhesus, sons of Muses, are Gods; unless, perhaps, a marine marriage takes precedence of one on land. If these are not Gods, because they are not worshipped anywhere, how can the others be? Consider, therefore, whether it is to the merits of the men, and not to their divine rank, that such honours are paid; as you also, Balbus, seemed to say. But, how can you, if you include Latona, refuse to count Hecate a Goddess, who was the daughter of Asteria, sister of Latona? Is she too a Goddess? We have seen her shrines and altars in Greece. And, if she is, are not the Eumenides also? And, if they are Goddesses, because their temple is in Athens, and among ourselves—as I understand it—Furina's grove; then the Furies are Goddesses—the detectives, I suppose, and avengers of crime and wickedness. But, if the Gods are so constituted as to take an interest in human affairs, Nascio must also be regarded as a Goddess; for, when we visit the temples in the district of Ardea, we usually sacrifice to her; and, as she presides over the child-births of matrons, she is called Nascio, from the births. If she is a Goddess, all those are Gods, that you have enumerated—Honor, Fides, Mens, Concordia—Spes also, Moneta, and all that we can imagine; and, if this is not admissible, neither is the doctrine from which all these have resulted.

19. 'What reason can you give—if those Gods exist whom we worship and have recognised—why we should not place Serapis and Isis in the same class? And, if we do that, why

should we reject the Gods of foreigners? We must, then, reckon as Gods, oxen and horses, ibes, hawks, asps, crocodiles, fishes, dogs, wolves, cats, and various other beasts; and if we reject these, we must reject also the system in which they originated. What next? Is Ino—named Leucothea by the Greeks and by us Matuta—to be called a Goddess; though she was the daughter of Cadmus? And shall Circe and Pasiphae, the daughters of Sol and Perseis, daughter of Oceanus, not be included in the number of Gods? Our colonists of Circeii, however, scrupulously worship Circe. Do you, for that reason, call her a Goddess?

'What answer will you give to Medea, who was descended from two grandfathers, Sol and Oceanus, her father Æetes and her mother Idyia; and to her brother Absyrtus, whom Pacuvius calls Ægialeus? The former name, however, occurs more frequently in ancient writings; and, if these are not Gods, I fear what may become of Ino: for all these come from the same source. Are Amphiaraus and Trophonius to be Gods? Our tax-farmers—as there were in Bœotia some consecrated lands exempt under the Censor's law—denied that any were Gods who had formerly been men. But, if these are Gods, so, without doubt, is Erectheus, whose temple and priest we have seen in Athens; and, if we make him a God, how can we hesitate respecting either Codrus or the others who fell fighting for the freedom of their country? and, if this is not admissible, neither are the other instances, from which these result, to be accepted. And yet, it is easily understood that, in most communities—for the purpose of encouraging heroism, so that all the best men may confront danger, in the service of the State—the names of gallant men are hallowed by the distinction of divine immortality. It is on that principle that, in Athens, Erectheus and his daughters take rank as Deities. There is also, in Athens, a temple of the Leontides, called the Leocorion. The people of Alabandæ, for instance, worship Alabandus, by whom that city was founded, more devoutly than any of the first-class Gods; and, when among them, Stratonicus, with the same wit that he displayed on many occasions—when some one obtrusively asserted that Alabandus was a God, and that Hercules was not—replied, "Then, may Alabandus be offended with me, and Hercules with you!"

20. 'As to those inferences, Balbus, which you drew from the heaven and the stars—do you not see how far they may

go?—that the sun and moon are Gods, one of whom the Greeks call Apollo and believe the other to be Diana. But, if the moon is a Goddess, Lucifer also, and the other planets, will attain the rank of Gods; and, consequently, the fixed stars also. But, why should not the phænomenon of the Bow be classed among the Gods? It is certainly beautiful; and, for the reason that it is a wonderful sight, is said to be the daughter of Thaumas; and, if its character is divine, what will you do with the clouds? Because the Bow itself consists of clouds in some degree tinted, and one of them is said to have produced the Centaurs. But, if you reckon the clouds among the Gods, changes of weather must certainly be included; for they are hallowed by the ritual of the Roman people. Therefore, showers, rain-clouds, storms, and cyclones must be regarded as Gods. Our generals, in fact, when going to sea, have been in the habit of sacrificing to the waves.

'Besides, if Ceres is so named from *gerendo*—for so you said—the earth itself is a Goddess and is so esteemed. For, what else is Tellus? If the earth is, so also is the sea, which you called Neptune; and therefore, rivers and fountains. Accordingly, Maso of Corsica consecrated the shrine of Fons, and in the Augurs' ritual, we find Tiberinus, Spino, Anio, Nodinus, and other names of adjacent rivers. So that, either this principle will have extensive application, or, we will admit none of them, and that unlimited system of superstition will not be accepted. Nothing of this sort, therefore, is to be admitted.

21. 'For that reason, Balbus, I must refute those, also, who assert that those Gods, whom we all elaborately and devoutly worship, are translated from human life to heaven, not actually but conventionally. In the first place, the theologians—so called—reckon three Jupiters, of whom they say that the first and second were natives of Arcadia—one, the son of Æther, from whom Proserpina and Liber were descended; the other, the son of Cœlus, who is said to have produced Minerva, whom they represent as the originator and inventor of war—the third, a Cretan, son of Saturn, whose tomb is found in that island.

'The Dioscuri, also, are named in various ways among the Greeks. The first group of three, called the Anakes— Tripatreus, Eubulus and Dionysus—born in Athens, and sons of Jupiter the first and Proserpina: the second group

of two, Castor and Pollux, sons of Jupiter the third and
Leda: the third group are named by some, Alcon, Melampus
and Tmolus, sons of Atreus, who was the son of Pelops.

'Still further—the first group of four Muses, Thelxinoe,
Aæde, Arche, and Melete, were daughters of Jupiter the
second: the second, of nine, daughters of Jupiter the third
and Mnemosyne: the third, of the same names and number
as the next preceding, daughters of Pierus and Antiope, and
by the poets usually called Pierides and Pieriæ.

'And, as you said that Sol was so named as being the only
one—how many of them are mentioned by theologians! One
of them is the son of Jupiter, and grandson of Æther:
another, the son of Hyperion: a third, son of Vulcan, son of
Nilus, whose city the Ægyptians believe to be that called
Heliopolis. The fourth is he to whom, in the heroic age,
Acantho is said to have given birth in Rhodes; father of
Ialysus, Camirus and Lyndus: the fifth, who is said to have
begotten Aceta and Circe in Colchis.

22. 'There are also several Vulcans. The first, son of
Cœlus, from whom and Minerva came that Apollo under
whose protection ancient historians believe Athens to be:
the second, a son of Nilus—Phthas, as the Ægyptians call
him—whom they regard as the guardian of Ægypt: the
third, son of Jupiter and Juno, who is said to have conducted
a forge in Lemnos: the fourth, son of Mænalius, who occupied those islands near Sicily which are called Vulcaniæ.

'One of the Mercuries is the son of Cœlus and Dies:
another, the son of Valens, who in his underground existence
is identified with Trophonius: the third is the son of Jupiter
the third and Maia, from whom and Penelope they say that
Pan was born: the fourth is a son of Nilus, whom the
Ægyptians considered it unlawful to name: the fifth, whom
the natives of Phanæa worship, who is said to have slain
Argus and consequently taken flight to Ægypt and taught
the natives laws and writing. This one the Ægyptians
call Thoth, and by the same name the first month of the
year is known to them. Of the Æsculapii the first was the
son of Apollo, worshipped by the Arcadians and said to have
invented the probe and first bandaged a wound. The second
was the brother of Mercury the second. He is said to have
been struck by lightning and buried at Cynosuræ: the third
was the son of Arsippus and Arsinoe, whom they assert to be
the inventor of cathartic medicine and the extraction of

teeth; and his tomb and consecrated grove are to be seen in Arcadia, not far from the river Lusius.

23. 'Of the Apollos the most ancient is that whom I have just mentioned as the son of Vulcan and protector of Athens: the second, the son of Corybas, and born in Crete, whose contest with Jupiter himself for that island is matter of tradition: the third, the son of Jupiter and Latona, who is said to have come from the Hyperboræi to Delphi: the fourth, known in Arcadia, and called by the natives Nomios, as they say that from him they received their laws.

'The Dianas also are many. The first was the daughter of Jupiter the third and Proserpina, and said to be the mother of the winged Cupid: the second, better known, who was, as we have heard, the daughter of Jupiter the third and Latona: of the third, the father is said to have been Upis, and her mother Glaucé. The Greeks call her by her father's name, Upis.

'We have many Dionysi: the first, a son of Jupiter and Proserpina: the second, a son of Nilus, said to have founded Nysa: the third, a son of Cabirus, and said to have ruled Asia as king, in whose honour the Sabazia were established: the fourth, a son of Jupiter and Luna, to whom the Orphic rites are supposed to be dedicated: the fifth, a son of Nisus and Thyone, by whom the triennial festival is believed to have been instituted.

'The first Venus is the daughter of Cœlus and Dies, whose temple we see in Elis: the second, born of the sea-foam, of whom and Mercury we are told that the second Cupid is the son: the third, a daughter of Jupiter and Dione, who was married to Vulcan; but, of her and Mars Anteros is said to have been born: the fourth, a Syrian and daughter of Cyprus, who is called Astarte and reported to be married to Adonis.

'Of the Minervas, the first was that whom I mentioned above as the mother of Apollo: the second, a daughter of Nilus, whom the Ægyptians of Sais worship: the third, I mentioned above as a daughter of Jupiter: the fourth, a daughter of Jupiter and Coryphe, daughter of Oceanus, whom the Arcadians call Coria and the inventor of four-in-hand teams: the fifth, daughter of Pallas, who is reported to have killed her father for attempting to assault her, and represented wearing anklets of wings. The first of the Cupids is called the Son of Mercury and Diana: the second, of Mercury and

Venus: the third, who is also Anteros, the son of Mars and the third Venus.

'All these and the like are collected from the old Greek legends, to which you perceive that objection must be made; so that religion may be redeemed from confusion. Your sect, however, not only fail to refute; but even sanction them by explaining the relation of every detail. But, let me return to the point whence I started on this digression.

24. 'Do you think that any more ingenious argument is needed for the refutation of this doctrine? For we see that intellect, faith, hope, virtue, honour, victory, safety, concord, and others of this class, have the quality of things, but not of Gods; because they either exist in ourselves—such as intellect, faith, hope, virtue, concord; or, are desirable for us—as honour, safety, victory. Of such things I perceive the utility; I see also their portraits consecrated; but why any quality of deities should exist in them, I shall under*stand,* when I discover it.

'In this class is to be included Fortune especially, which nobody can imagine apart from inconstancy and recklessness, which are certainly not suited to a God. Besides, what pleasure does that interpretation of fables and derivation of names afford you?—Cœlus mutilated by his son—Saturn imprisoned by his son. These and similar legends you uphold in such a manner that the inventors of them would seem to be not only not insane, but actually wise. In the derivation of names, however, you are pitiably astray—Saturn, because he fed himself—*Saturaretur*—with years: Mavors, because he effects great revolutions—*Magna vertit:* Minerva, because she diminshes or threatens—*Minnit* v. *Minatur:* Venus, from her advent—*Venit*—to all: Ceres from *gerendo!* How dangerous a habit! Many names you will find unmanageable. What will you do with Vejupiter? What with Vulcan? Although, as you suppose Neptune to be derived from *nando*—swimming—there will be no name of which you cannot trace the origin from a single letter; and, in this respect, you seemed to be more at sea than Neptune himself.

'Zeno first: then Cleanthes, and afterwards Chrysippus, took much and very superfluous trouble in giving the meaning of allegorical apologues, and explaining the reasons why several names were so formed. But, when you do the same, you will certainly admit that the fact is far different from what is commonly supposed—that, for instance, what are called Gods, are qualities of things and not divine forms.

25 'This mistake extended so far that not only was the title of Gods actually given to mischievous things, but even rites of worship instituted. The temple of Febris, for instance, we find consecrated on the Palatine, and that of Orbona, near the temple of the Lares, and an altar to Misfortune on the Esquiline. Let all such ignorance, then, be banished by philosophers: so that, when arguing about the immortal Gods, we may use language worthy of them; for I have a belief of my own respecting them, but no inducement to agree with you. You say that Neptune is an intelligent consciousness pervading the sea, and give a similar account of Ceres; but, any such intelligence in sea or earth, I am unable not only to understand, but even to guess. So that, in order to understand the existence of Gods and their attributes, I must inquire of some other source than your doctrines.

'Let us now examine what comes next. First, whether the world is governed by the wisdom of the Gods; and secondly, whether they provide for human interests; for these two are the remaining propositions of your division. These, if you have no objection, should, I think, be discussed more carefully.'

'It certainly meets my wishes,' said Velleius. 'For I look forward to more of the discussion, and agree fully with what has been said.'

Then said Balbus, 'I don't wish to interrupt you, Cotta, but let us choose another time: I will certainly bring you to make a confession; but——'

HERE a considerable portion of the original MS. has been lost, or, more probably, destroyed; containing all the discussion of the third article of the Stoic dogma—the Divine government of the world. The loss has been sometimes attributed to the early Christians, who may, perhaps, have mutilated the text, on the principle enunciated in the fragment rescued by Lactantius—'Non esse illa vulgo disputanda. Ne susceptas publicé religiones disputatio talis extinguat'—which is true in all times and places. Logic has always been fatal to superstition; and too often superstition has retaliated, with heavy interest, upon logicians. It would seem, however, that, even on that principle, the Pagan fanatics would be more likely than the Christians to have celebrated the *Auto da fè*, or, at least, to have had a stronger motive; for they considered this essay, and that on divination, only one degree less dangerous than the New Testament: and Cardinal Baronius states that, under Diocletian, an application was made to the Senate for a warrant to burn these works of Cicero together with the Bible: which was actually done. The champions of the Christianity which he so nearly approached, appear to have regarded Cicero with more indulgence; if we may judge by the remarks of a learned critic commenting upon this essay—A.D. 1720—who says: 'If reason alone cannot always discover truth, it can at least go so far as to detect falsehood; which Cicero has proved. He found the light of nature enough to refute atheism and idolatry. He did not, indeed, know enough to establish true religion; but he knew enough to confute Stoics and Epicureans, the only men who dared to stand up against St. Paul at Athens. Providence seems to have raised up Cicero to prepare the way for Christianity by exploding these two pernicious systems.' Cicero, however, did more than this, even 'by reason alone.' He marked the intrinsic and eternal distinction between right and wrong, which some Christian moralists have treated as a question of mere expediency, to be determined by hope of reward and fear of punishment. But this commentator, while disparaging human reason, is naturally unjust to Epicurus, who was not, any more than Cicero himself, an Atheist, and was as perversely misunderstood, as to his theology and doctrine of hedonism, as Bishop Berkeley was by the men of his time. He is unjust also to the Stoics, who, to an equal certainty, never taught or sanctioned idolatry, and in their system of ethics—as we learn from Epictetus and Marcus Aurelius—coincided very nearly with the austere sect of Christians generally known as Puritans. Most commentators, indeed, seem to have overlooked the fact that Cotta's argument, all through, is a logical *tour de force*, and not always strictly ingenuous; being, in some instances, open to the imputation of *ignoratio elenchi*—*i.e.*, non-recognition of the real question—a form of sophism that proves elaborately what no philosopher has ever denied, and refutes, with equal diligence, what no philosopher has ever asserted.

Another fragment saved by Lactantius is quoted in this form—'Primum, igitur, non est probabile eam materiam rerum unde orta sunt omnia, esse divinâ providentiâ effectam; sed habere et habuisse vim et naturam suam. Ut igitur faber, cum quid ædificatum est, non ipse facit materiam, sed ea utitur quæ sit parata, fictorque item cerâ, sic isti divinæ providentiæ materiam præsto esse oportuit, non quam ipse faceret, sed quam haberet paratam: quod si non est a deo materia facta, ne terra quidem, et aqua et aer et ignis a deo factus est.'

The argument here stated amounts to this—that, as it is more probable, than otherwise, that matter had always an independent existence, the Creator could not have made it, and could only have given it form and motion, as a human mechanic might do; and therefore, could not have created the world. Now, to any rational view of the question, the probability, of course, seems all on the affirmative side; and further, as the paragraph has no perceptible reference to the question in hand—the divine government of the world—and resembles mediæval rather than Ciceronian Latin, it may be reasonably doubted that it is genuine.

The question which it really raises, seems to be that of the interaction of mind and matter; and is so stated by the Abbé d'Olivet—'Si ce Dieu n'etoit absolument qu'une âme, de quelle maniere s'uniroit-il au monde?' Socrates, in his long conversation with Timæus, and, in modern times, Leibnitz, have treated this question very ingeniously; but, it has never been conclusively answered. We can never get beyond the external phænomena.

26. '"It shall never end in that way—a mighty contest is involved.

That I should ever supplicate them with such humility!

Why should I?"

'Does she not seem to reason well enough, and plan a guilty ruin for herself? But how ingeniously she says,

'"He that will have what he desires, finds success proportioned to his energy."'

A line which is the planter of all evil—

'"With hostile purpose he has, this day, given me imprisonment,

From which I will let loose all my vengeance and give him ruin—

Sorrow for me; woe to him: ruin for him; exile for me!"

'Of course, such intelligence as this, which, you say, is given to man alone by the divine power, lower animals do not possess. Do you not see, then, how kindly we are treated by the Gods? And the same Medea, in flight from her father and her country—

'"When her father approaches, and she is preparing to be overtaken—

In that interval, she slays the child and severs limb from limb;

And all through the fields scatters the fragments, to this end,

That, while her father gathered the dispersed body of his son,

She might, herself, escape—that grief might hinder his pursuit,

And that she might make safety for herself by fratricide."

'She did not lack intelligence proportioned to her guilt. Well, then? Did not he who prepared a tragical banquet for his brother, exercise his reason on various plans?

'"A greater task for me—a greater mischief to be organized, To shock and crush his hateful heart."'

27. 'Nor yet must he be omitted,

'"Who was not content with having seduced a wife."

Of whom Atreus properly and most truly says:

"'This in a serious case, I deem the greatest danger,
The pollution of royal consorts—
The adulteration of race, and mixture of blood."'

'But, how artfully he treats that subject, who sought a crown by adultery!

'"To this," he says, "I add the prodigy sent by the father of Gods
To me, a warning and the safeguard of my throne.
That Thyestes dared to steal from out the palace—
A lamb bright amid the flocks with golden fleece,
In which he had a faithless wife to aid him."

'Does he not seem to have practised the worst of crime, not without perfect intelligence? Nor, indeed, is the drama alone fertile of such crimes; but ordinary life of what are almost worse. Every man's house knows: the forum, the Senate-hall, the park, the allies, the provinces, all know that, as good is effected by reason, so by reason are crimes committed; the former by few and seldom; the latter constantly and by a large majority; so that it were better that no reason at all had ever been given to us by the immortal Gods, than given with such fatal results. As it would be better not to use wine at all, because it is now and then beneficial, but most frequently injurious; than, in the hope of possible benefit, to risk a manifest injury; so, I am not sure that it would not have been better for mankind that this swift movement of thought, ingenuity, craft, which we call reason, should not be given at all, than bestowed so liberally and abundantly; since it is ruinous to many, and beneficial to very few. Wherefore, if divine intelligence and will has provided for man, so far as it has bestowed reason on him; it must have provided for those only whom it has gifted with true reason; and these, if any, we know to be very few. As it is not likely that provision has been made by the immortal Gods for only a few; the inference is, that it has not been made for any.

28. 'This argument, that the best provision has not been made for us by the Gods, because many make a perverted use of their bounty, you usually meet in this way—that many persons make a bad use of their properties, but cannot be said, for that reason, to receive no benefit from their ancestors. Can any man deny that? or, what analogy is there in the comparison? Dejanira, for instance, had no intention of hurting Hercules, when she gave him the tunic dyed in the

Centaur's blood; nor did he mean to do a service to Jason of Pheræ, who opened his abscess with a sword, which the physicians were unable to heal; for, many persons, while intending to hurt, have done good; and, while meaning kindness, have done mischief; so that it is not from what is given that the intention of the giver can be inferred: nor, if the receiver uses it wisely, has the giver, for that reason, bestowed it with a friendly hand. What sensuality, what avarice, what crime, is either designed without premeditation, or accomplished without mental impulse and reflection—that is, reason? All opinion is reason: true reason, if the opinion is right: perverse if the opinion is wrong. But, from God we simply have reason; but its quality, as good or bad, from ourselves. Because it is not, as an estate is inherited, that reason is given to man by the bounty of the Gods; for what would they give in preference, if they meant to injure him? What germs could there be of injustice, intemperance, and cowardice, if reason did not supply means to those vices?

29. 'The heroic characters, Medea and Atreus, have been just now mentioned as projecting impious crimes on a designed and matured plan. Well? the trifles of comedy? Have they not always sufficient association with reason? Does not that character in the Eunuch reason sensibly with himself?

' " What am I to do, then? She locked me out—she calls me back.
Will I come?—No!—Not even if she begs for it."

The other, however, in the Synephebi, is ready, in academic fashion, to argue against the popular belief, when he says that,

' " Amid the strongest love and the sorest penury,
It is a pleasure to have a close-fisted, crusty father,

Harsh to his children, who neither loves nor cares about you."
And supports this paradox with arguments.

'He argues, further, that an indulgent and open-handed father is an inconvenience to a son in love:

' " For I don't at all know how to deceive him, so as to gain anything from him;
Or, what deception or contrivance I can bring to bear on him,
So much has his indulgence defeated all my plans, deceptions, and mystifications."

Well then? All those devices, contrivances, deceptions and mystifications? Could they exist independently of reason? Precious gift of the Gods! It enabled Phormio to say:

'"Show me the old gentleman! for I have all my plans arranged in my head."

30. 'However, let us leave the stage and turn to the bar. The Prætor comes into Court. To decide what? Who set fire to the Registry. What crime is less likely *to be discovered*? And yet, Q. Sosius, a first-class Roman Knight, from the Picene district, had confessed that it was his act. Who falsified the public records? That, too, L. Alenus did, when he forged the signatures of the six commissioners. What could be more clever than that man? Study other trials—those respecting the gold of Tolossa, the conspiracy of Jugurtha. Go back to events of older date—the impeachment of Tubulus for receiving money for a judicial decision. Turn to recent trials—for incest, under the Perducean Act: then, these crimes of daily occurrence—the daggers, the poisons, the embezzlements—the trials repecting wills even, under the new act. Then, the indictments upon this charge —"I assert that by your aid and instigation theft has been committed." All the numerous sentences upon fraud, guardianships, trusts, partnerships, commissions, and all the other breaches of faith in sales and purchases, hiring and letting. Next, public decrees on personal affairs under the Lætorian law—then, the procedure against fraud, a besom for all sorts of malice, which our friend C. Aquillius introduced; and fraud Aquillius defines, as consisting in pretending one thing and doing another. Are we to suppose, then, that all this crop of mischief has been produced by the immortal Gods? For, if the Gods have given reason to man, they have *given* malice, which is a versatile and deceptive principle of mischief: they have also given fraud, wickedness and other evils, none of which could be designed or accomplished without intelligence. I wish, therefore—as that old woman wishes:

'" That in the Pelion forest, by the axe
That pine-tree cut had not been felled to earth "—

That the Gods had not bestowed that cleverness on man; for the few who use it well, are still constrained by those who use it badly: and they who employ it perversely, are countless; so that, this heavenly gift of reason and forethought would seem to be given to man for dishonesty and not for goodness.

31. 'But, you argue, now and then, that it is the fault of men, not of the Gods: as if a physician were to lay the blame on the severity of the disease, or, a pilot on the violence of a storm. Though these are only men, still they would act absurdly. Who would have employed you—some one might say—if such were not the case? Against a God we can argue still more freely. You say that the fault is in the defects of human nature. But you might have given to man such intelligence as would make the defects and the fault impossible. Where, then, was there room for a mistake on the part of the Gods? We leave our estate, for instance, in the hope of a fortunate succession, in which we may possibly be disappointed; but how can a God be mistaken? May he be mistaken as Sol was, when he placed his son Phaeton in his chariot; or, Neptune, when Theseus destroyed Hippolytus, though he had from his father Neptune the chances of three wishes? These are legends of the poets; but we desire to be philosophers, and to state facts instead of fables. And yet, even these Gods of the poets, if they knew that those gifts would be fatal to their sons, would be supposed to be wrong in their concessions. And, if it is true, as Ariston of Chios used to say, that philosophers do mischief to those who perversely interpret lessons of wisdom—because spendthrifts might issue from the school of Aristippus, and ascetics from that of Zeno; and then, if their hearers were likely to go away with those faults, because they perverted the lessons of philosophers; it were better that philosophers were silent, than do mischief to their hearers. On the same principle, if men apply to dishonesty and malice the intellect bestowed with good intention by the immortal Gods, it were better that it be not given to mankind.

'As, if the physician knew that a patient, who was recommended to take wine, would take it too strong and die presently, would incur serious blame; so, is that providence of yours open to censure, for bestowing intellect on those whom it knows to be likely to use it perversely and mischievously. But, perhaps, you say that it did not know—I wish you could. But you won't venture; for I know what importance you attach to its name.

32. 'This argument, however, may be now closed; for, if

stupidity is, in the unanimous opinion of all philosophers, a greater evil than all the misfortunes of property and person, if weighed against it; and, if no man attains wisdom, we are all involved in the worst of evils, though you say that the best provision has been made for us by the immortal Gods. Because, as it is all the same whether no one is well, or none can be well; so I cannot perceive what difference it makes whether no man is wise, or no man can be so. We have been dwelling too long upon a most evident fact. Telamon sums up in one line the whole question, why Gods neglect men:

'" For, if they cared for them, the good would be happy and the vicious would suffer,"

which is not so at present.

'It was their duty, in fact, to make all men good if they took thought for mankind. Failing that, they should at least have provided for the good. Why, then, did the Carthaginians, in Spain, crush the two Scipios—most gallant and excellent men? Why did Hannibal slay Marcellus? Why did Cannæ cut off Paullus? Why was the person of Regulus exposed to the barbarity of the Carthaginians? Why did Maximus witness the death of his son, the past consul? Why did not his own house shelter Africanus? But these are ancient instances of which there are many more. Let us examine more recent cases! Why is my uncle, P. Rutilius, a most harmless, and, at the same time, most learned man, in exile? Why was my friend Drusus murdered in his own house? Why was the Pontifex Maximus, Q. Scævola, a model of temperance and prudence, slain in presence of the statue of Vesta? Why had C. Marius, the most treacherous of men, power to order the death of Q. Catulus, a man of eminent respectability? The day would be too short if I wanted to mention good men who were unfortunate, and equally so, if I were to enumerate criminals who prospered. Why, for instance, did Marius die so happily of old age, in his seventh consulship, in his own house? Why did Cinna, the most cruel of men, enjoy absolute power so long?

33. 'But he was punished, you will say. It would have been better that he were hindered and prevented from putting to death so many eminent men, than that he should be punished. With the worst tortures of punishment, Q. Varius, a most mischievous man, met his death. If it was

because he compassed the death of Drusus by the dagger, and of Metellus by poison, it were better that they should be saved than Varius punished for his crimes. For eight-and-thirty years Dionysius was the absolute ruler of a most wealthy and flourishing State. For how many years did Pisistratus, who preceded him, hold the same position in the leading city of Greece? But Phalaris and Apollodorus, you will say, were punished. It was after torturing and murdering many victims! Many pirates, even, are often punished; and yet we cannot say that more of their prisoners than of themselves are not cruelly put to death. We have heard that Anaxarchus, a pupil of Democritus, was butchered by a king of Cyprus; that Zeno of Elea suffered death by torture. Why need I speak of Socrates, over whose death I sometimes shed tears when reading Plato? Do you not see, then, that in the opinion of the Gods, if they do regard human interests, all distinctions are effaced?

34. 'Diogenes the Cynic used to say that Harpalus, who was considered a successful pirate in those days, gave evidence against the Gods by living so long in that condition. Dionysius, whom I mentioned above, was on his voyage to Syracuse, after plundering the temple of Proserpina; and, while keeping his course before a fair wind, laughed and said, " Do you see, my friends, how prosperous a voyage is granted to men guilty of sacrilege?" And when, by keen observation, he thoroughly understood that fact, he continued under the same conviction; for, when he landed in Peloponesus and visited the temple of Olympian Jupiter, he stripped him of a golden tunic of considerable weight with which King Gelon had furnished him out of the spoils of Carthage, and even made a joke of it, saying that a golden garment was an incumbrance in summer, and cold in winter, and clothed him with a woollen shawl, observing that it was suited to all seasons of the year. He also ordered the golden beard of Æsculapius, in Epidaurus, to be removed; as it was not proper that the son should be bearded, while the father, in all his temples, was beardless. He also commanded the removal of the silver tables from all the shrines; because as they were, according to the old Greek fashion, inscribed "To the Good Gods," he said he wished to avail himself of their goodness. He took away, also, without hesitation, the gold statuettes of Victory, and the cups and crowns, which were held in the extended hands of the idols; and said that he accepted, but did not

take them—as it would be folly to refuse to accept favours from those to whom we prayed for them, when they offered and gave them. And they say, still further, that he exposed all those treasures in the forum, and sold them by auction; and, when he had collected the money, issued an edict that whatever consecrated property anyone had should be restored to its proper temple by a certain day. Thus to impiety towards the Gods, he added dishonesty towards men.

35. 'This man, then, neither Olympian Jupiter struck with a lightning-bolt, nor Æculapius wasted away to death with a miserable and chronic disease; and, dying of dropsy in his bed, he was taken to the pyre; and that power which he had won for himself by crime, he transmitted as an heir-loom to his son, as if it were normal and constitutional.

'I discuss this topic reluctantly, as it seems to imply a license for crime; and would be correctly so understood, were not the intuition of right and wrong, independently of any divine principle, a heavy responsibility, by the removal of which all distinctions are levelled. For, as neither a household nor a State can be regarded as arranged under any system of government, if there are neither any rewards for merit, nor penalties for crime; so, there is certainly no divine government over men, if there is no distinction between good and evil.

'But then, the Gods overlook the smaller details, and pay no attention to the farms or vineyards of individuals; nor, if blight and hail do any mischief, does it come under the notice of Jupiter; Kings even do not attend to every trifling particular. This is what you say; as if I had just now complained respecting the Formian farm of P. Rutilius, and not of the loss of his life.

36. 'And, in fact, all men regard this question in this way; that they receive from the Gods external benefits—vineyards, corn, olive-gardens, abundance of grain and other produce, and, in short, all the comfort and prosperity of life; but for moral excellence no man has ever acknowledged himself indebted to God. And, to all appearance, truly; because, for that excellence we are duly praised, and are justly proud of it; which would not be the case if we considered it a gift from God, and not from ourselves. But, when obtaining any advancement in political or private life, or, if we have gained any accidental advantage, or averted any

evil; then we attribute nothing to our own merit. Has any man ever been thankful to the Gods for being a good man? But he thanks them for being rich, influential and prosperous: and accordingly, they call Jupiter best and greatest, not because he makes men just, and temperate, and wise; but, because he renders them healthy, prosperous, powerful and wealthy. No man has ever promised a tenth to Hercules, in case he should become wise; and yet Pythagoras, when he made some new discovery in geometry, is said to have sacrificed an ox to the Muses; that, however, I do not believe, since he would not even to Delian Apollo offer a victim, lest he should stain the altar with blood. But —to come back to the question—this is the verdict of all men; that success is to be sought from God, and wisdom gained from ourselves. Although we dedicate temples to Mens, Virtus, and Fides, we still perceive that these qualities dwell in ourselves. So that, as Democritus used to say, the good fortune and prosperity of reprobates disprove all might and power of Gods.

37. 'Occasionally good men do experience favourable results: these we seize and illogically attribute to the immortal Gods. But when Diagoras, who is known as the Atheist, arrived in Samothrace; and a friend said to him, "You, who think the Gods indifferent to human affairs—do you not perceive from all these paintings, how many have, by their vows, escaped the violence of the weather and arrived safely in port?" "Just so," he said, "for those are never painted who have been shipwrecked and perished at sea." And further, when, during a voyage, the crew, alarmed and frightened by rough weather, said that they deserved it, for having taken him on board with them; he showed them many others in similar distress, and asked if they believed that a Diagoras was on board the others also. The truth is, in fact, that with reference to good or bad fortune, it makes no difference what you are, or how you may have lived. The Gods, he says, do not take notice of everything; nor do Kings even. What analogy is there? For, if Kings are wilfully negligent, it is a serious fault.

38. 'A God, however, has no excuse for ignorance. And yet you defend him successfully when you say that the power of the Gods is such, that, if one escapes the penalty of his guilt, that penalty is exacted from his children, or grandchildren, or descendents. Wonderful justice of the Gods!

Would any community tolerate the framer of a law to such an effect, that the son, or grandson, should be condemned, if the father or grandfather had been guilty?

> "What limit to the deadly strife of the Tantalidæ
> Can be set? or, for the death of Myrsilus
> What full atonement to vengeance can be made?"

'Whether the poets have perverted the doctrine of the Stoics, or the Stoics lent their authority to the poets, *it is* not easy for me to say; for miracles and crimes are mentioned by both. For instance, neither he whom the iambics of Hipponax hurt, nor he who was wounded by the verses of Archilochus, brooded over his pain, as inflicted by God rather than created by his own consciousness; nor, when we contemplate the profligacy of Ægisthus or Paris, do we trace its origin to God, while we can almost hear the voice of the crime; nor do I consider the recovery of many patients not to be attributed to Hippocrates, rather than to Æsculapius; nor would I say that the discipline of the Spartans was given to their country rather by Apollo than by Lycurgus. It was Critolaus, I say, who overthrew Corinth, and Hasdrubal who ruined Carthage. It was these two who put out those eyes of the sea coast; and not any vengeance of God, whom you describe as incapable of anger. But he surely had power to help and preserve cities of such influence and importance.

39. 'You are, yourselves, in fact, in the habit of asserting that there is nothing that God cannot perform, and without an effort; for, as the limbs of the human body move without any effort, by their own tendency and impulse; so, can all things be formed and changed and set in motion by the will of the Gods; and you assert, not in the spirit of superstition or dotage, but on a scientific and consistent principle —that the matter of which and in which all things consist, is all changeable in form and substance; so that there is nothing that cannot, however suddenly, be made of it or transformed; and that, of all this, divine providence is the designer and controller; and this can, therefore, accomplish whatever it pleases and wherever it moves. Therefore, it either knows not what it can do, or neglects human interests, or is unable to determine what is best. It takes no care of individual men. It is not strange that it should disregard communities also. Does it not care for these? Not even

nations and peoples. But, if it overlooks these also, what wonder is it that all mankind should be deemed unworthy of its notice? But, how can you, at the same time, say that the Gods do not attend to everything, and believe that dreams are dispensed and sent severally to men by the immortal Gods? I address this question to you; because the theory of the truth of dreams is your own: and you also maintain the propriety of undertaking vows—of course, if individuals make vows, then the divine intelligence listens to individuals. Do you see, then, that it is not so busily employed as you supposed? Grant that it is widely distributed, traversing the heavens, surveying the earth, and controlling the sea; why does it permit so many Gods to do nothing and live in idleness? Why does it not employ some idle Gods in the administration of human affairs; as they are stated by you, Balbus, to be innumerable?

'This is about all that I had to say respecting the attributes of Gods; not with a view to abolish them, but to show you how indefinite they are, and difficult to be explained.'

40. When Cotta had so spoken, he concluded. Then, said Lucilius, 'You have indeed, Cotta, assailed rather violently that doctrine of the Stoics, which had been most reverently and wisely established by them, respecting the providence of the Gods; but, as evening is drawing near, grant us some other day, to reply. For I have a controversy with you for religion and home; for the temples and shrines of the Gods, and for the walls of the city, which you priests assert to be consecrated, and protect the city more carefully with its religion than with its walls; all which I consider it a crime to desert, so long as I can breathe.'

Then said Cotta, 'I do, indeed, wish to be answered, Balbus, and I would rather discuss than decide the questions I have raised, and I am quite sure that I can be refuted by you.' 'Of course,' said Velleius, 'believing, as he does, that dreams are sent to us by Jupiter; and yet, even these are not so unreal as the Stoic doctrine of the nature of Gods.' After this conversation, we separated on the understanding, that, to Velleius, Cotta's argument appeared to be the more convincing; while to me that of Balbus seemed more nearly to approach the truth.

NOTES.

CH. 13. *Nullum corpus immortale.* All this elaborate argument involves an evident *ignoratio elenchi;* because it is not for the visibly and universally transient body that immortality has ever been claimed —except, perhaps, by those modern Pythagoreans, the Rosicrucians— but for the immaterial spirit that survives it. This obvious distinction is, all through the discussion, kept out of view as persistently as if none of the disputants had ever read Plato. In the simple and chain syllogisms also, which form the *reductio ad impossibile*, we find, here and there, a false premiss. It is said, for instance, that whatever suffers pain, is also liable to death; which is untrue; because, in all æras of high civilization, the mind, which is the immortal element in our constitution, suffers more than the body. Of all animals, man is the most gratuitously cruel; and, when the fashion of the time prevents him from torturing the bodies of his fellow-creatures, he expends his superfluous malice upon their minds, for which there is no law to punish him. The whole argument, in fact, is more or less gratuitous; and Cotta wastes a large amount of logic in refuting what no philosophers ever asserted or believed.

Ch. 15. *Societas et communitas*, etc. Here we have the doctrine afterwards expanded in the utilitarian philosophy of Hobbes, Hume, and Bentham. The argument of the leviathan is this—man's natural condition is a state of war, *i.e.*, of rivalry and competition. In this no moral element exists. To this war it is consequent that nothing is intrinsically unjust. In war, force and fraud are the cardinal virtues. As there is no element of morality or justice in man, so long as he is unsocial, and no society but the union of individuals, we can have no right or wrong, except that which positive law, resulting from that union, and consequent punishment make such. Hume says that, if we imagine a condition of society in which every man could have, in abundance, all that he desired, there would be no competition for anything, and the ideas of justice and honesty would have no existence.

To this argument of Hume's the obvious reply is, that the question relates not to the result of impossible conditions, but to what is most probable and most reasonably to be, *à priori*, expected under the existing system of divine government.

THE END.

BILLING AND SONS, PRINTERS, GUILDFORD.

CPSIA information can be obtained
at www.ICGtesting.com
Printed in the USA
LVOW13s1014190518
577801LV00008B/44/P

9 781377 091082